CUSTER SURVIVOR

The End of a Myth
the Beginning of a Legend

JOHN KOSTER

Published in the United States by
Chronology Books, an imprint of
History Publishing Company LLC
Palisades, New York

ISBN-10: 1933909-03-X
ISBN-13: 978-1933909-03-5
LCN: 2009936668
SAN: 850-5942

    Koster, John P., 1945-
       Custer survivor : the end of a myth, the beginning of
    a legend / John Koster.
       p. cm.
       Includes bibliographical references and indcx.
       LCCN 2009936668
       ISBN-13: 9781-933909-03-5
       ISBN-10: 1-933909-03-X

       1. Finkel, Frank. 2. Little Bighorn, Battle of the,
Mont., 1876. 3. United States. Army. Cavalry, 7th--
Biography. 4. Soldiers--West (U.S.)--Biography.
I. Title.

    E83.876.K56 2010   973.8'2'092
                         QBI09-600167

Printed in the United States on acid-free paper

9 8 7 6 5 4 3 2 1

First Edition

Contents

Acknowledgments

Five people were absolutely vital in the development and writing of *Custer Survivor*. My wife Suzy, as our American Indian friends call her, adopted into both the Lakota and the Crow tribes, won me the confidence of many people not inclined to look with favor on anyone whose name and appearance bear any resemblance to "Custer." They liked her much better. My daughter Emily, an honors graduate of Princeton, as is her husband, convinced me that many people would be interested in the story and stepped in for some rapid-fire computer and editing expertise. Minjae Kim turned up a number of key documents, just as she has researching stories for *America's Civil War* and *Wild West,* and provided back-up in computers and editing. My son John Frederick Koster, better known as LJ, provided a vital video and some last-ditch computer expertise. The story that I learned my computer skills at Neander Valley Community College is apocryphal, even if he claims it's true.

White people who assisted include the fifth member of the A Team, Don Bracken, whose expert editing skills turned what was originally a work of argumentation into an adventure story based on responsible scholarship. Don also contributed to what was already a staggering inventory with some facts and photographs much too important to leave out. All five of these people were utterly vital to the work.

With all the development and writing completed, two people were vital to putting it all together into the attractive book it is. My thanks to Angela Werner for her wonderful interior design. She has made a book replete with documentation an integral and easy part of the reading process, and a special thanks to Angela too, for putting up with all my late additions. And a warm thanks to Bob Aulicino for his work of art that is the cover. It caught the essence of *Custer Survivor*. It does everything required of a cover.

Pride of place among those not involved on a day-to-day basis must go to Professor Louise Barnett, author of *Touched By Fire*, who analyzed the data and wrote the introduction; to Greg Lalire of *Wild West*, who published the original story; to Jeffry Wert, author of *Custer*, who found the research plausible; to Scott Cross, archivist at the Oshkosh Public Museum and guardian of the Finkel File, and to the Oshkosh Public Musem Director, Brad Larson; and to John Doerner and Sharon Small at the Little Big Horn Battlefield Memorial who found photographs and maps with great efficiency and dispatch. Dr. Thomas P. Lowry, MD, John Ydo, former Wyckoff police chief, Keith Killion, former chief of detectives in Ridgewood, Astrid Baker, MLS, and Sandra Luebking, editor of *Forum*, helped authentic the handwriting. Glenn Hoefler of the Glen Rock Library, Mike Shinn of the Ridgewood Library, and Tim Murphy of the Fair Lawn Library helped order rare books and pamphlets. Mike took the author photo. John Smythe of Glen Rock Mail & More handled emergency scanning. George Kush (registered Blackfoot Indian) provided useful observations and facts about the West of the 1870s. Wallace Black Elk (Oglala Lakota), a collateral relative of Crazy Horse, John Eagleshield (Hunkpapa Lakota), a collateral relative of Sitting Bull and John Grass, Leonard Crow Dog, medicine man of the Sicangu (Brule) Lakota, and Tom and Suzy Yellowtail of the Crow, who knew Custer's old scouts, offered me great personal insights into the original Americans. E.W. "Doc" McRoberts and Carol Bennett, Western whites who liked and respected Indians, were extremely helpful.

Members of the Finkel family and their friends who provided priceless vintage photographs include Milton "Mickey" Koch, Rebecca "Reba" Koch, Faye Rainwater, Mike Watson, and friends from Dayton including Shellie McLeod, Mary Byrd, and the excellent staff of the Columbia County Courthouse headed by Chief Deputy Auditor Naedene Shearer. Their warm hearts and warm sense of humor and their intense efficiency in getting things done were both immensely impressive.

Finally I would like to mention Buddy LaMonte, Pedro Bissonnette, and Tina Manning Trudell. *Mitakuye oyasin. Pilamiya.*

One long sword escaped, though; his pony ran off with him and went past our lodges. They told me about it at Chicago. I saw the man there, and I remembered hearing the squaws tell about it after the fight.

—Rain-in-the-Face, Sioux Chief

Preface

Custer's Last Stand, the Battle of the Little Big Horn, on June 25, 1876, is the most famous small military engagement in American history, partly because the U.S. Department of the Army reported that there were no survivors, a contributing factor that lends much to the mythology that has enveloped the event.

But military battlefield records are often incomplete. The chaos of battle, and the destruction the human body frequently experienced in the intensity of battle which often disallowed identification, assured that reality. That reality is no more evident than was in the record-keeping relative to the Battle of the Little Big Horn.

Contrary to the popular myth, there was a survivor. His survival is confirmed by forensic evidence, much of it revealed in this work for the first time. In a case of inheritance or criminal proceeding, such evidence would make his identity a foregone conclusion.

Flying in the face of a myth supported by unquestioning adherents might be construed by some to be a daunting task, for there is no more difficult obstacle to overcome than that of the closed mind. But in an open society such as ours there are many who are always looking for new answers to old problems and old, unanswered questions.

The evidence presented here does, indeed, answer that old, un-answered question: Was there a survivor of the five companies with George Armstrong Custer at the Battle of the Little Big Horn? The answer in this book is very positive. Yes, there was a survivor, the Second Sergeant of Company C.

Introduction

As long as wars have been fought, there have been war frauds, those counterparts of heroes who step forward to claim unearned glory. They said they were shadowy assassins in the Phoenix program in South Vietnam, flyers belonging to the Lafayette Escadrille in World War I, escaped POWs, and anything and everything else that could be brandished as a credential of bravery and toughness. Most were men who had done nothing to merit their country's gratitude, either not serving at all or compiling a record of dysfunctionality in the military. Some had genuinely earned medals but wanted to burnish their war records even more.[i] The desire for "stolen valor" has not even spared the privileged: a number of politicians have been exposed as falsifiers of their military records, and a well-known historian was found to have regaled his college classes with stories of his exploits in the Vietnam War—although he spent the war in a library at West Point. No doubt for every man who had been revealed as an imposter, many escape public exposure, retailing their phony wares only to friends and family.

The Battle of the Little Big Horn was tailor-made for such fraudulent battle claims. Notorious from the time a stunned world heard the news, the clash between the Army and the Sioux and other

Plains Indians was a traumatic national event that changed nothing historically but delivered a blow to the self-confident psyche of a nation celebrating its first centennial. Since Custer's force had been killed to the last man, there was no Army survivor to report on its final moments, a condition that led to endless dispute over every aspect of Custer's Last Stand. Eyewitness accounts of the American Indians who had fought there were discounted by white Americans as unreliable or impossible to make sense of. Differences of language and culture seemed insurmountable in that day and age. Moreover, many of the warriors who later settled on reservations thought it would be politic to deny any knowledge of, or responsibility for, the deaths of United States soldiers.

Given the lack of certain knowledge of Custer's final movements after the five companies under his command had separated from the rest of the regiment, it was inevitable that men would come forward to claim the unique role of sole survivor, a position that no one else could easily challenge. In the quarter-century after the battle, and well into the twentieth century, such claimants were plentiful: Theodore Roosevelt said that he had met or heard of fifty such, while the distinguished Western historian, Brian Dippie, collected over seventy such stories. Others have reported even higher totals. But unlike the majority of the men who have appropriated a false role in the Vietnam War, the "sole survivors" were laying claim to a battle that had quickly become renowned.

Transported by railroad to Billings, Montana, tourists made the remote battlefield a popular attraction: anniversary commemorations were quickly established, and battle buffs subjected every detail of the clash to intense scrutiny. Whereas many modern-day frauds have found their unsubstantiated claims readily believed, the sole survivors quickly encountered skepticism. Each had his brief moment of publicity before his story was rejected and the tale-teller returned to deserved obscurity. This has not been the case with Frank Finkel.[ii] His story persisted because it was more believable. For Dippie, Finkel had "perhaps the soundest case ever advanced by a 'Sole Survivor'." Because he maintained that he had simply outrun the Indians, he gained "in credibility what he lost in drama."[iii] Dippie believed that the earlier historian, Charles Kuhlman, had found Finkel's story persuasive because it fitted so nearly into his own hypothesis about the battle. Nevertheless, when Dippie revisited the issue of sole survivors in an essay published in 1981, he cautioned that dismissing all such claims "is a bit premature."[iv]

There are many issues at play in a determination of Finkel's claim to sole survivor status. First of all, it has been viewed by many with disbelief because of inconsistency of identity. After all, the Finckle who enlisted in 1872 used the first name of August and the birthplace of Berlin, Prussia. And Frank Finkel's second wife, Hermie, always said that her husband had enlisted under the name Frank Hall.

Contesting any accepted historical "fact" requires a researcher who can see the situation in a new light and who then goes on not only to reinterpret it but to discover new evidence. Long familiar with the part of the country where the battle took place, John Koster had a sudden illumination about Frank Finkel based on a detail about a horse—a dead Seventh Cavalry horse found at the confluence of the Rosebud and Yellowstone Rivers that had always intrigued battle buffs. In then-Lieutenant Edward Godfrey's first account of seeing this animal (1892), no mention was made of its color. Only much later did Godfrey reveal that it had been a sorrel, a color that identified it as belonging to Tom Custer's C Company. This was Finkel's company as well. The mysterious dead horse was thus the right color and was in the right place to be seen as the horse Finkel said carried him away from the battle and which he later shot.

Two other clues contributed to the story: Rain in the Face, a warrior indisputably at the battle, had said that one cavalryman escaped, and Charles Windolph had been unable to find his good friend Finckle's body when he expressly looked for it on the battle-field—although Daniel Kanipe said that he had seen Finckle's body. How to choose between these opposed accounts? Eyewitness testimony is notoriously contradictory: forensic evidence needed to be uncovered to make the strongest case.

The test, one might say, is history, or rather, the process necessary to assemble the pieces of what occurred into a coherent narrative that could take its place in the history of the battle of the Little Big Horn. As skillfully unraveled and then reconstituted by Koster, Frank

Finkel's story has been stripped of the misleading material generated by Finkel's own attempt to bolster his credentials when he enlisted, and by his second wife's misguided version of his past. These distortions have led many to dismiss Finkel as merely another fraud, albeit one who did not seem to fit the pattern of other sole survivors. With the falsehoods removed and hiatuses filled in by Koster's painstaking investigation, Finkel's story now makes sense: in Koster's reconstruction of his subject's life, the Frank Finkel who asserted in 1920 that he had survived the Last Stand, and the August Finckle who enlisted in the army in 1872 were one and the same. The real American-born and German-speaking Finkel, only eighteen, plausibly adopted the persona of a twenty-seven year old German-born Prussian officer as a means of enhancing his status. But Prussian records indicate that there was no suitable August Finckle to be found in German birth or American immigration records. Two American-born August Finckles unearthed by Koster lived and died in their native states without any military status.

As for the parts of the story that can never be verified—Finkel's sojourn in the wilderness and subsequent wanderings—lack of evidence neither supports nor discredits his narrative. He did not specify what his injuries were, so we have no basis for assuming that he was "gut-shot" and hence doomed because he describes one bullet wound as "in the side." A bullet could have punctured the skin without penetrating any organ, as its quick closure would indicate.

Eventually returning home after his ordeal at the Little Big Horn, and no doubt fearful of being prosecuted as a deserter, Frank Finkel spent the next forty-four years as a solid citizen of Dayton, Washington, a family man and prosperous landowner. Some of the publicity about imposter survivors may have reached him, along with their subsequent unmasking, but he seems to have had no need of fortune and no desire for fame. When he did speak out publicly in 1920, it appears to have been impulsively at first rather than planned. He never embellished or romanticized the battle as other "sole survivors" and journalists did, nor did he seek either publicity or money.

Over the years a view of the battle has reified among battle buffs, precluding any substantive alteration. But in dismissing the idea that all sole survivor stories must be fake, they forget that one accepted story of an almost-survivor very similar to Finkel's: that of the cavalryman who, according to his Indian pursuers, would have gotten away had he not suddenly put his pistol to his own head.[v]

Research uncovers records, but it takes patience and imagination to fashion the data into a plausible factual account. Like any proposed revision of a story enshrined by time and tradition, Koster's telling needed to account for those parts of the story that didn't fit while bringing a new perspective to a well-known claim. This has been his achievement: he focused on forensics, hunting down Frank Finkel's signature on his first wife's will and comparing it to the enlistment signature of "August Finckle." A number of experts have now agreed that the signatures are most likely those of the same person. To resolve the identity problem, Koster contacted Germany where no records supported the existence of "August Finckle." He brought his own Germanic thoroughness to the pursuit of every detail of the story and every myth that has grown up around it. Because of his effort, we can be more certain than at any time in the past that there was indeed a sole survivor of the Last Stand and that his name was Frank Finkel.

—Professor Louise Barnett,
Professor of American Studies and English,
Rutgers University
Author of *Touched By Fire*

Notes

[i]A huge number of such cases have been collected by B.J. Burkett and Glenna Whitley in *Stolen Valor: How The Vietnam Generation Was Robbed of Its Heroes and Its History*, (Dalla, Verity Press, 1998)

[ii]I will use "Finkel" throughout except for explicit references to August Finckle. "Finckle" was the spelling used by the man we now know as Finkel when he married for the first time. But late nineteenth century records show that the spelling eventually stabilized as "Finkel." This kind of orthographic instability is not unusual for the time.

[iii]Brian W. Dippie, *Custer's Last Stand: The Anatomy Of An American Myth*, Missoula, University of Montana Publications in History, 1976, 86-87.

[iv]"Why Would They Live?" Thoughts on Frank Finkel and Friends in *Custer And His Times*, ed. Paul A. Hutton (El Paso: Little Big Horn Associates, 1981) n 225. Dippie's essay, pp. 209-228, provides a good review of the sole survivor literature.

(v)Walter M. Camp, "Interview With Foolish Elk," September 22, 1908, *Custer In '76: Notes On The Custer Fight,* ed. Kenneth Hammer, new ed. (Norman: University of Oklahoma Press, 1990), 199. "He saw no man get away but had heard four different eye witnesses tell of one soldier who rode through the Indians on a very swift white horse which they could not catch. They told that after chasing him for a mile or two the soldier drew his pistol and killed himself. This they could not understand, because the man's horse was swifter than theirs and was continually getting farther away from the pursuers."

Part One

The Man Who was Frank Finkel

CHAPTER ONE

Drums in the Night

June 24, 1876

The valley of the Little Big Horn River shook to the pounding of drums and the falsetto quavering wail of Lakota warriors, augmented by the melodious full-voice singing of the Cheyenne and the giggling of girls. Just one week before these Indians, once ill-fed at their government agencies with beef and bacon that was often rancid, coffee mixed with dirt and flour hardened to plaster-of-Paris, had defeated a large force of pursuing soldiers and enemy Indians at the Rosebud River, and sent the Army back to lick its wounds. Now it was time to dance.

With the drums beating, the singing, the girls flirting, and the testosterone surging, it must have seemed surrealistic and other-worldly to a young man, the present world and the Rosebud forgotten.

"My mind was occupied mostly by such thoughts as regularly are uppermost in the minds of young men," said Wooden Leg, a Cheyenne. "I was eighteen years old, and I liked girls. It seemed that peace and happiness was prevailing all over the world, that nowhere was any man planning to lift his hand against his fellow man."[1]

Lakota and Cheyenne dances were ladies' choice: the girls, working in gaggles, cleared the dance floor of sagebrush and weeds and then roamed in blushing, giggling groups, teasing young men by throwing berries at them and asking them to the dance. The purpose was courtship. Both tribes had a dread of incest, and a camp the size of the one on the Little Big Horn was a splendid opportunity for girls to find marriageable men. Shy by themselves, but bold in groups, the girls joked with the young men and asked them to the dance, while their mothers often worked to provide food during the intervals. The mothers were also involved in courtship: "fort marriages" to transient soldiers generally left the girls abandoned with half-breed children, and the Lakota and Cheyenne esteemed chastity and found outright prostitution repugnant.

Once in awhile, the Lakota girls would hold a "virgin dance" where those girls who were virgins, or claimed to be, would promenade in a graceful, upright prance and any boy who claimed otherwise had the chance to throw dirt on the virgin imposter. If the boy told the truth, the embarrassed girl dropped down several clicks in the marriage market but remained unpunished. If he was a liar—you could tell by looking at both sets of eyes—the girl and her friends swarmed over him and beat him up.

The courtship dance at the Little Big Horn was a rousing celebration, most of the people in the vast camp of Lakota and Cheyenne had never seen so many Indians, or so many girls and boys. While the young people danced, the girls traipsed upright to reveal their beauty and elegance and, at least, suggest their chastity. The young men gyrated wildly, showing off the limber strength that would make them great warriors and great hunters, and great providers.

Some young men, though, were scoundrels of opportunity. There were three ways for a Lakota warrior to obtain what he wanted, a present of horses or other valuables to the future bride's father, an elopement after which the bride's family accepted what had happened, and "teepee crawling," obtaining girls' favors by crawling into their teepees, with the girl's permission, and hoping the rest of the family didn't wake up. The girls much preferred to elope and rarely liked a teepee crawler.[2]

Mothers of marriageable girls stayed up all night to keep their eyes on the dancing—and their daughters—or stayed awake at their teepees cooking meals of meat and *tunsipi,* Indian turnips, one of the rare vegetables in the Plains Indian diet and a seasonal treat.

While the mothers watched, the fathers drummed: each drum was an instrument, with a drumhead of two or three feet, beaten with synchronized strokes by four male drummers with drumsticks in a rhythm that simulated the human heartbeat. Each "drum" was a group of close friends, older warriors or older men who no longer danced, but offered music while they shared fellowship, while their wives kept an eye on the girls to make sure they behaved. Married women sometimes sang the high, quavering tremolo at the end of each dance to cheer on the dancers and drummers.

The dance thundered on through the night while young men roamed from camp to camp, danced to exhaustion, then stopped off where married women with eligible daughters fed them *tunsipi* and roasted meat and sized them up as sons-in-law. Then the young men got up and danced again.

The dancers never touched. Girls and boys danced in groups of friends with a sense of fascination, excitement, and power at seeing so many Indians in one huge encampment. Most danced until dawn. One young man, Wooden Leg, was so exhausted that he reached his own teepee at sunrise but fell asleep outside the flap.

"People were dancing around fires all over the village," the Lakota Black Elk remembered. At 13 he was too young to be court-ing. "We boys went around from one dance to another, until we got too sleepy to stay up any more."[3]

The next morning, the dancers, the drummers, and the women with daughters in their high teens and 20s were all asleep. Some of the younger boys got up for a swim, and the women whose daughters were too young for courtship, or whose children were all boys, took the youngsters and headed for the hills in search of more turnips.

Most others sought shelter from the heat of the day inside the lodges, where the shade and the air circulation made the 100-degree temperatures of a Montana summer bearable.

Black Elk, too young to dance, was able to get up by mid-morning and went for a swim, but he had an odd sensation that wasn't due to last night's exhaustion. "I did not feel well; I felt queer. It seemed that something terrible was about to happen."[4]

Notes

[1] Marquis, Thomas, *Wooden Leg, a Warrior Who Fought Custer,* pages 214-216.

[2] Hassrick, Royal B. *The Sioux: Life and Customs of a Warrior Society.*

[3] Neihardt, *Black Elk Speaks,* page 108. Many older Lakota people also told Mildred Fielder about the all-night dance.

[4] *Ibid.*

Photos following Chapter One courtesy of the Library of Congress.

American Horse – Hunkpapa

Big Beaver – Cheyenne

Black Elk – Oglala Sioux

Bobtailed Horse – Cheyenne

Brave World – Cheyenne

Crazy Bear – Oglala Sioux

Crow King – Hunkpapa

Dull Knife – Northern Cheyenne

Feather Earring – Minneconjou

Flying By – Minneconjou

Flying Hawk – Oglala Sioux

Fool Bull – Brule Sioux

Gall – Hunkpapa

Goes-to-War – Oglala Sioux

Gray Whirlwind – Hunkpapa

He Dog – Oglala Sioux

Hollow Horse Bear – Brule Sioux

Hump – Minneconjou

Ice – Cheyenne

Iron Hawk – Hunkpapa

Iron Thunder – Minneconjou

John Grass – Sihasapa Sioux

Julia Face – Oglala Sioux woman

Kicking Bear – Oglala Sioux

Lame White Man – Cheyenne

Little Hawk – Cheyenne

Little Soldier – Minneconjou

Little Big Man – Sioux

Louis Dog – Cheyenne

Low Dog – Oglala Sioux

Miss Spotted Horn Bull – Sioux woman

Moving Robe – Sioux Hunkpapa woman

No Flesh – Hunkpapa Sioux

One Bull – Hunkpapa

Rain-in-the-Face – Hunkpapa

Red Horse – Minneconjou

Scabbard Knife – Sioux

Short Bull – Brule Sioux

Shot-in-the-Eye – Minneconjou

Sitting Bull – Hunkpapa Sioux

Standing Bear – Minneconjou

Stump Horn – Cheyenne

Tall Bull – Cheyenne

Touch the Clouds – Oglala Sioux

Two Moon – Cheyenne

White Frog – Cheyenne

White Shield – Cheyenne

White Bull – Minneconjou

Wooden Knife – Sioux   *Wooden Leg – Cheyenne*

Chapter Two

The Attack

June 25, 1876

From the top of the hill, it looked like a sure thing. He would attack after mid-day. Lt. Col. George Armstrong Custer had planned to attack the huge Indian village at dawn the following morning with support from another column, but the situation had changed. Sergeant William Curtis, sent back to look for a provision pack dropped by the mule train, found some stray Indians helping themselves to the hardtack biscuits. Curtis had been spotted, he thought.

Custer decided to attack immediately, before the Indians could escape. But there was unease and uncertainty in the ranks. Earlier, when Custer's Indian scouts summoned him to look over the village from an elevated crag called the Crow's Nest, they pointed out the pony herd below "like worms in the grass." Custer couldn't see the horses. His vision had lost its acuteness, perhaps from the gonorrhea he had contracted in New York City while a cadet at West Point.[1] The Indian scouts and Lieutenant Charles Varnum, the Army officer in charge of the scouts, could see the pony herd with their naked eyes. Custer couldn't see the huge pony herd with binoculars.

But peering down into the big Indian village on the Little Big
Horn River from a height of 180 feet, Custer saw women and children and dogs—and no men. The situation was clear to him: the
Sioux and Cheyenne warriors must be off hunting antelope. The
Indian women digging turnips and the children playing with the
dogs could be rounded up without serious losses to either side and
used to coerce the men into returning to their agencies.

But some of his scouts didn't think it would be that simple; they
were uneasy. So were the troopers of the 7th Cavalry who waited
with a shifting sense of unease. But Custer needed a quick victory for
redemption. A Washington scandal in which Custer gave testimony
against the entrenched powers had brought him painful career difficulties.

Having lost his chance to command the whole expedition
against the hostile Indians, he had to pull strings with his Army
mentor, General Phil Sheridan, to retain field command of even the
7th Cavalry.

The command of the three-part expedition was given to General
Alfred Terry, a fortunate choice, for Custer. He had interceded for
Custer to serve as commander of the 7th Cavalry under his own
supervision and Custer got the 7th. He would lead one of the three
wings.

As he looked down on the village, Custer knew it was another
day in a long string of uneasy days for the men of the 7th Cavalry.
Everyone felt it, including Custer, but for him the excitement of victory was greater.

C Company, under Captain Tom Custer and Second Sergeant
Frank Finkel, first felt that unease as they set out from Fort Abraham
Lincoln in Dakota Territory on May 17, 1876, when an optical illusion in the cloud formations overhead made it look as if the forward
companies of the regiment were riding right into the sky, the first of
many foreboding omens later reported about the 7th Cavalry on the
Sioux expedition of 1876.

Although he was anxious for an engagement with the Sioux
and Cheyenne, Custer wasn't planning a wholesale massacre. As he
surveyed the Indian village below him he probably gave little thought
to a decision he had made earlier.

Unaware that a week earlier, on June 17th, General Crook had been attacked and soundly hammered by Crazy Horse and the Sioux on the Rosebud, Custer had refused the offer of General Terry to take four companies of the 2nd Cavalry, three Gatling guns, and a three-inch Rodman cannon from the late-arriving Colonel John Gibbon's command for his own attack formation.

Custer separated the 7th Cavalry from Terry's mixed force of cavalry and infantry for the final phase of the attempt to locate and smash the Sioux. This would be his day. Custer didn't know about Crook's upset and reversal on the Rosebud, but he had few doubts about his own ability. Wasn't he the youngest general in the Civil War, and the victor over the Cheyenne in 1868 on the Washita? He was filled with inexhaustible energy and self-confidence.

And he had the need for a quick and glorious triumph. Today.

The attack formation was taking place. Tom Custer's C Company was to lead a wing with L Company following and I Company in reserve. E and F were over to the left with George Yates leading E.

It happened fast. The order was given. "Mount up!"

Second Sergeant Frank Finkel was riding side-by-side with his close friend, Sergeant Daniel Kanipe, just behind Captain Tom Custer and First Sergeant Edwin Bobo, in the lead company. Finkel was six-foot-one, the tallest soldier in the regiment, and his sorrel gelding was laboring to keep up.

"I don't think I can make it—my horse is giving up," Finkel yelled to Kanipe, who, at five-foot-eleven, was the second tallest man in C Company.

"Come on, Finkel, if you can," Kanipe shouted back.[1] Kanipe's moon face was pale and his hazel eyes were wide with fear. Kanipe looked to be as worried about himself as he was about losing Finkel. They'd fought the Sioux once before, at the Yellowstone in 1873 when they were still privates, and they trusted each other under fire.

Tom Custer cantered back as the advance slowed down, took one look at Finkel's wheezing horse, and gave Kanipe, the duty sergeant, the orders to take to the rear.

"Tell McDougall to bring the pack train straight across to high ground," Captain Tom Custer said. "If packs get loose, don't stop to fix them, cut them off. Come quick. Big Indian camp."[2]

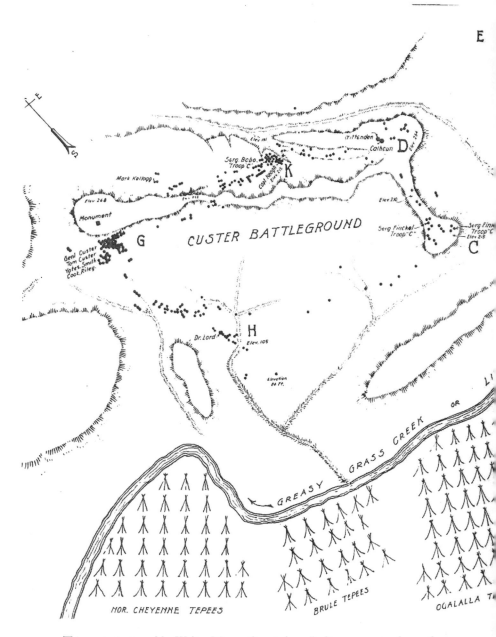

This map, prepared by Walter Mason Camp from Indian accounts, shows the terrain Finkel would have ridden over in his escape from Custer's Last Stand. Figure C marks Calhoun Ridge, where C Company was shot to pieces at the beginning of the battle. "Finckel" marks the space where a body "mutilated very badly" was mistakenly identified by Sergeant Kanipe—but not by Charles Windolph,

Finkel's best friend, who went back to look for Finkel's body and couldn't find it. The real Finkel's runaway horse carried him downhill and turned at the verge of the Little Big Horn River, past the Hunkpapa (here Uncapapa) camp, where Indian women saw "one long sword escape(d): according to Rain-in-the-Face. (Map courtesy of Little Big Horn Battlefield National Monument Museum)

The Seventh Cavalry on the march with three .50-caliber Gatling machine guns, a three-in breechloading Rodman cannon, and 150 supply wagons. This photograph from the 1874 Bla Hills expedition shows what the regiment would have looked like on the first stage of the mar toward the Little Bighorn in 1876.

Sergeant Kanipe swung his roan sorrel away from C Company and galloped to the rear. The last words he heard Lt. Col. Custer say were: "Boys, hold your horses, there are plenty of them down there for us all."[3] A young Crow Indian scout swung out just after Kanipe and also took off for the rear.

The sight of the village stunned everyone. Nobody had expected such a large encampment. Custer's adjutant, a big Canadian named W.W. Cooke with magnificent dark mutton-chop whiskers, handed another quick note to Trumpeter Giovanni Martini, a short, hardened Italian who was serving as Custer's orderly. Martini took off to the rear.

A few hundred yards after Martini turned back carrying the message, Frank Finkel on his struggling horse rode up on two C Company men with horse troubles, Privates Peter Thompson and James Watson. Thompson's horse was blown and standing still, gasping, and Watson's horse had fallen down on one side with exhaustion and was struggling to get back up. Watson furiously kicked the horse to get him on his feet again, Finkel sat calmly on his horse looking on, then suddenly, the poor animal gained his feet with a groan, and Finkel passed on with a rush to overtake C Company.[3]

C Company moved down toward the ford of the Little Big Horn at the bottom of the hill. When they came up on the village, it was looking bigger and bigger all the time. Lips were dry and throats were tight. The companies came into line. Finkel could see a few women and kids moving around among the hundreds of teepees. The horses were nickering and snorting when they saw the village and smelled the Indian ponies and the wood smoke, sweet grass, and wet leather.

Suddenly two green troopers on scared horses broke loose from the company and rode right through the stream. The troopers and horses disappeared into the village and the Indian women started to scream and duck. A warrior stepped out of a teepee holding a Winchester. Finkel and others in C Company could hear the thud of the troopers' Colt .45 revolvers and the sharp crack of Winchesters and Henrys as the Indians killed them. More warriors poured out of the teepees. A handful of warriors ran to the ford on foot and started shooting, while the women, some of them dragging their children, ran away for the trees.

C Company balked. The size of the village and the rapid gunfire from the Indians, more and more each passing moment, left the men dumbfounded. Finkel looked around for orders. Sergeant Bobo was looking around too. Lieutenant Harrington was scared to death, his cheeks grey beneath the dust and sweat. But where was Captain Tom Custer?

The Indians kept pouring out of the lodges and turned toward the stream while the women and kids ran the other way. It was like the sudden opening of what appeared to be an empty nest of a swarm of hornets, Finkel thought. His body went cold and his flesh started to creep.

The Indian women were singing a high warbling cry that sounded like summer locusts, almost like little bells ringing, to encourage the men. It was the tremolo and it made Finkel's flesh run cold—they weren't trying to escape after all....

Thwack!—a puff of dust and blood flew up from one trooper's gingham shirt and he slid off his sorrel without a sound except for the thud when he hit the sandy ground. Dust spots were kicking up all over. Another man grunted at a *thwack* and looked down at blood gushing over both sets of fingers.

"Oh my God..." He slid out of the saddle and landed on one shoulder, kicking. Up the line, a gray C Company hat flew backwards through the air. Another trooper slipped off his horse. A horse was hit and shrieked—Bobo's horse. The Indians downhill were screaming and Finkel could hear the women singing the tremolo down in the village. The reddish dirt was dancing and jumping between the clumps of sagebrush.

Finkel yanked his Springfield carbine out of the scabbard. He drew a bead on a warrior down by the river. The carbine jolted back in his hand and the bare steel barrel cracked him in the forehead. He saw red—shock, then blood. Finkel's sorrel gelding lurched as a bullet hit his flank and the horse took off down the slope. A bullet smacked into Finkel's shoulder like a sledgehammer and he reeled in the saddle. His foot jerked in the stirrup—another bullet in the leg.[5] The remnants of the company headed downhill with bullets kicking up dust around troopers and horses.

Finkel's sorrel gelding screamed a high-pitched shriek as the shock of the bullet wore off. He could feel the horse's heart pounding through its sides as the sorrel ran frantically downhill to get away from the pain in his flank. Finkel stayed balanced on his horse by instinct and habit as the horse turned hard left at the low, clear river, and ran past a blur of teepees on the far side of the Little Big Horn.

As in a dream, he saw a couple of Indian women looking at him. They seemed curious. He leaned forward on the sorrel's neck, dazed with shock. Blood dripped on the reddish-brown mane. The noise of the shooting, the war whoops and the tremolo seemed to fall away behind him as he drifted into a dazed, semi-conscious state, just barely feeling the horse beneath him and the pain in his shoulder, his leg, and his forehead.[6]

Notes
[1]Jeffery D. Wert, *Pg. Custer,* pages 34-35.
[2]Graham, Col. W.A., *The Custer Myth,* page 249, Account of Sergeant Daniel Kanipe. Sergeant Kanipe's height and appearance from Old

Military Record, National Archives, Washington, DC and photo from Little Big Horn Battlefield Memorial Museum. Walter Mason Camp and Mari Sandoz also report Sergeant Finkel's presence, as does the *Bismarck Tribune* front page story of the "massacre."

[3]Account of Peter Thompson from the *Belle Fourche Bee*, Belle Fourche, South Dakota, December 1913. Thompson, a native of Scotland and a soldier for about a year in 1876, later won the Congressional Medal of Honor for bringing water to the wounded on Reno Hill, but didn't follow the Custer brothers and Finkel down to the river after his horse gave out. Kanipe confirmed this part of his story. Walter Mason Camp, dean of Seventh Cavalry and Indian interviewers, found some other parts of Thompson's narrative fantastic, but accepted—with the corroboration of Kanipe, other soldiers and Indian scouts—that Thompson was kept out of the battle by horse trouble and not by cowardice. Thompson died in 1928 and was buried with full military honors.

[5]Graham, Col. W.A., *The Custer Myth,* page 249, Account of Sergeant Daniel Kanipe.

[6]Finkel File, Oshkosh Public Museum. All 1920s newspaper accounts, most of them undated due to clipping, report his injuries consistently.

Photos following Chapter Two courtesy of the Library of Congress.

Captain Thomas Custer

Sergeant Jeremiah Finley

Sergeant Daniel Kanipe

Trumpeter Giovanni Martini

Sergeant Charles Windolph

Lt. Charles Varnum – Chief of Scouts

First Sergeant Edwin Bobo

Corporal John Briody

Lt. James Calhoun

Lt. William Cooke – Adjutant

Lt. James Crittendon

Lt. Charles DeRudio

Lt. Francis Gibson

Lt. Edward Godfrey

Lieutenant Henry Harrington

Captain Myles Keogh

Dr. George Lord

Corporal Daniel Ryan

Lt. Algernon Smith

Lt. James Sturgis

Private William O. Taylor

Private Peter Thompson

Lt. George Wallace

Captain George Yates

Bloody Knife – Arikara

Bobtail Bull – Arikara

Boy Chief – Arikara

Curly Head – Arikara

Little Brave – Arikara

One Feather – Arikara

Soldier – Arikara

Red Bear – Arikara

Red Star – Arikara

White Man Runs Him – Crow

White Swan – Crow

Young Hawk – Arikara

Chapter Three

Surviving After the Battle

Finkel woke to a flaming pain in his shoulder and his leg. His sorrel, Ginger, was still running, trying to get away from the pain in his flank where the gunshot wound had plowed a red furrow through his reddish coat. The country was different now, more grass and less sagebrush and red earth.

Finkel's head throbbed with pain. He knew it resulted from the Indian's bullet that had struck the butt of the carbine. The bare steel barrel had pivoted into his forehead. His whole left side was on fire and he felt numb and stiff. His frightened horse, wheezing and heaving, galloped furiously. Finkel didn't have to use his spurs.[1]

Night was falling when he reached a stream smaller than the river. Finkel tried to dismount, his foot pushed against the stirrup and the pain shot up his left leg like an enflamed spear. Fire seemed to blaze in his chest but his thirst forced him to get off the horse. He trod the soil in agony barely able to walk, but the bone wasn't broken, he came to realize.

He dipped up a hatful of water from the little steam and winced as the shift in weight put pressure on his burning leg. He put the

soaking, dripping gray hat, now black with wetness, to his lips. The
water stank of bitter alkali. He shut his eyes tight and threw the water
on his face, then tried to drink the acrid stuff. He vomited, coughing
up the tainted water out of a dry, thirsty throat. His sorrel snorted
and wouldn't touch the water.

Frank climbed back into the saddle. His eyes bulged with pain
as he put his weight on his left leg. He nudged his horse on at a walk.
The Indians were far behind him now, or so it seemed. His thoughts
were on his thirst and the pain in his shoulder and leg.

A few miles on, after dark, he came to another stream. Ginger
snorted—more alkali. Frank took a chance. He clambered down out
of the saddle. The pain was a dull silent roar in his whole left side. His
lips were cracked with thirst. He was light-headed, but his leg burned
like a flaming log and when he got to the stream, the water still stank
of sharp alkali. He threw some more water in his face and swung
into the saddle, clumsily gripping the pommel with his right hand
because of the burning in his left chest. He spat out words—violent
epithets—but he couldn't reduce the pain in his leg.

The moon was rising when he came to the third stream. He was
swaying in the saddle. His horse sniffed the water, lowered his head,
and started to drink. Frank braced himself and dismounted, the leg
still burning. He could feel his thick, wet blood oozing from his leg
when his foot pushed against the stirrup.

He limped to the dark, rippling water, took off his hat and
dipped up a hatful. The water was sweet and pure. He drank with
deep relief. He slumped down and slept.

The next couple of days were a blur of the dull pain of riding,
punctuated by the blazing agony of dismounting and remounting.
He rode Ginger eastward, by instinct, perhaps back to Fort Abraham
Lincoln, or maybe his home in the Chicago flophouses or perhaps,
his childhood home on a farm in rural Ohio.

On the second day he arrived at a river he assumed was the
Rosebud and followed it. He drank its murky water after allowing
the mud to drop and settle at the bottom of his tin cup. Nothing,
he must have thought, would ever taste as sweet as the water in the
wilderness at that third stream.

Ginger, weakening from his wound, stopped frequently to rest and graze, his head drooping. Finkel knew the sorrel was dying, probably from exhaustion as well as the shock of the wound in his flank.

Finkel had a haversack full of hardtack squares and a sack of oats the 7th Cavalry had issued just before the assault march. He munched on them as he traveled, chewing the hard plaster-like crackers. When he offered Ginger a hardtack cracker, the sorrel just let it fall from his mouth; the horse didn't care about food any more. Frank took a bagful of oats, gathered some in his fingers and placed them under Ginger's mouth, but Ginger wouldn't eat the oats. His lips seemed to kiss Frank's hand. He was alive from habit.[2]

Toward sundown, Finkel found a prairie chicken sitting on her nest. He limped up on the fat little bird and shooed it away. The bird stomped at him and bristled, but backed off. He groped among the eggs, picked one up and stuffed it in his mouth. The egg was slimy, disgusting, He bent over and vomited. He left the rest of the eggs, the prairie chicken retaking its nest.

At night, the wilderness moved in on Finkel, the yip-yip-yip and howling of coyotes ever present. The dried blood on his blue soft-wool trousers and his dark blue sergeant's blouse was hardening and he could still feel the blood oozing from his leg as he lay in the night.

On the middle of the fourth or fifth day, Finkel and Ginger came to the end of the Rosebud, where it met the Yellowstone River. Finkel dismounted and looked at the confluence of the two rolling rivers thinking that the world ahead was made of water. As he and Ginger stood side by side on the riverbank, the horse caved in and fell on one side with a thud and struggled to get up, but couldn't.[3]

Finkel, having grown up on a farm and being a trooper in the cavalry, knew horses, he knew Ginger was dying. He gave the horse's big head one last hug and ran his fingers through the coarse bristly mane to show Ginger he wasn't mad at him and still loved him. He slipped out his Colt .45 quickly, so he wouldn't have to think about it, and put the muzzle to the sorrel's forehead, right on the white diamond blaze, and pulled the trigger. The revolver bucked in his hand and the head dropped away, instantly lifeless. A thin trickle of blood dribbled down the white blaze on the horse's face.

Frank slipped the horse's bridle off in case he found another horse. He left the carbine with the shattered stock in the scabbard. The whole point now was to get away from the horse before he started to stink—and so he didn't have to look at him. He left quickly, not wanting to look at the dead Ginger, and set off up the river hoping for a steamboat.

As sundown approached, he heard a *pock, pock, pock* sound. Puzzled, he stopped abruptly and listened intently to the regular rhythm of the sound, knowing it had to be man-made. He was on the lower side of a rise. When he crested the hill he saw a white-bearded man in brown gingham shirtsleeves chopping wood next to a dilapidated shack. Finkel was relieved, deep in the wilderness, one white man by himself meant he was out of Indian country.

He was stiff and sore but he hunched his way down the low hillside and came up on the white man chopping wood.[4]

The man swung around like a shot.

"What the hell do you want...?" the man said, then ducked toward the shack and picked up a Winchester standing against a woodpile.

"I got shot..." Frank said. He was cautious ... uncertain. The man's voice had a Southern influence. People in the South had a deep dislike of the Boys in Blue but in the West soldiers were always welcome, especially in Indian country.

"Get the hell out of here," the man said, keeping the Winchester pointed at Frank's belly. Finkel's eyes rolled, his legs buckled, and his body fell to the ground.

When he awakened, Finkel was inside the shack lying on a rope bed across from a man he had not seen on his arrival. The man was clean-shaven, gaunt and pale, with reddish splotches on his pale white skin; his eyes appeared to be strangely alighted. Then he started to cough. As soon as Finkel heard the wet, stubborn cough, he knew the man was dying of tuberculosis.

"My name's Frank..." he said.

"I'm George," the man in the bed said.

"I'm Bill," said the man with the whiskers who had met Finkel outside the shack. "Let's look at your leg."

Frank pulled his blood-stained blue trouser leg out of his boot. Bill gave him a drink, then leaned down, pulled up the trouser leg, and stared at the blood-caked limb.

"Damn," said Bill "I think this leg had better come off."

"If I've got to die, I'd rather do it all in one piece," Frank said. [5] He looked down at the leg and saw a huge blue bruise around a black hole; a slight oozing flow of blood was centered in a dried blood crust. The bullet had missed the bone but the whole calf was discolored and starting to shrivel, hairs protruded out of the caked blood like brush tops after a river flood. Frank's stomach turned and he wanted to retch but he asked for a drink. The man gave him what appeared to be moonshine.

"Well, the slug has to come out anyway," said Bill "Better probe for it?"

"Give me another drink first," Frank said.

The man handed him another cup of moonshine and Frank tipped it back.

Bill rose up and picked up a pine branch from a corner store of wood, then whittled a stray slab into a long pointed sliver.

He started to probe in the leg wound while George watched, fascinated and horrified. Frank could feel Bill's hot breath on his leg. The sharp pain was relatively mild compared to the pain he had felt walking on the leg.

"It's started bleeding again…" Bill said.

"Let's boil up some pine pitch," said George. "That'll stop the bleeding once and for all." He gave out another rough, watery cough.

Bill got up right away. He was shaving the bark off some pine logs into a pot over the pot-bellied stove in the shack. The fire got the pine pitch bubbling. It was nice to be near a stove for a change, Frank through blearily… like old guys eating cheese and crackers and arguing about politics when the fields were frozen under the snow. In a strange vague way, it seemed like home.

Frank stretched out his leg and Bill poured the steaming pitch on the leg. The fire-like pain traveled up his leg and shriveled his crotch. Finkel blacked out.

When he woke up he wondered where he was.

George was sleeping in the bed next to him. Frank looked at the pale, splotchy face. It seemed to Finkel that he wasn't long for this world.

Then he felt something on his chest. Bill had placed a folded wad of cotton cloth stuffed with lint, smeared with bear grease, on the gunshot wound on his shoulder. The pain was dull in comparison to the fire he had felt in his leg. He could handle it, a couple of drinks would help too.

But who were these two men? Were they squatters, men living on unregistered land? Trappers? Whiskey traders? Frank knew better than to ask. People who left the States, America east of the Mississippi and Missouri Rivers, and moved into the Territories generally had something to hide, especially if they came out by themselves, without women and children.

Bill was okay, Frank thought. He gave him the same invalid's diet he gave his friend George: tin cup after tin cup of broth made of boiled bones. The stove was going all the time, filling the shabby cabin with the smell of broth. Bill also made *ponada*, crumbled bread boiled with canned milk and raisins or dried apples. He even had a nutmeg he grated into the *ponada*—made it taste good.

Frank was very weak at first, but as he got better, George weakened. Incessantly coughing and spitting blood intermittently, then wheezing fitfully in his difficult sleep.

One morning when Frank woke up, George was dead, having passed way during the night. Frank wasn't sure when he saw the still body, but when he touched George, his body was cold and stiff.

Finkel felt a chill and said the Lord's Prayer. Bill didn't cry but stared at his friend as if the world had come to an end.

"I think we better bury him…." Frank said.

"I hate to think of throwing dirt in his face," Bill said. "We've been friends a long time."[6]

Frank had been trying to walk around a little and had become somewhat familiar with the place; he'd seen some scrap lumber left over from the building of the shack.

"If you give me a hand, we can fix up some kind of coffin out of them boards," Frank said.

"Sure…" said Bill.

Bill had to do most of the work. Frank's chest was still sore from the gunshot wound and his arms were weak from the inactivity. They crudely constructed a pine box that covered George's face and upper body, the legs protruding when they put him in the ground. As Bill wanted, the dirt didn't land on George's face when they buried him.

Frank stood over him and said the Lord's Prayer and the 23rd Psalm, to himself. Bill stood looking forlornly at him.

"Let's make a cross," Frank said.

"I don't want no cross over him," Bill said. Frank was mystified, but he didn't argue about it.[7]

"We shouldn't just stick him in the ground with no marker at all," Frank said. "It don't seem right."

Finally, they got a rock and painted the initials G.W. on it. Frank couldn't figure why Bill didn't want a cross. Where he grew up, half the people were Irish and the other half were German and everybody wanted a cross, even if they never went to church.

Frank couldn't figure out what Bill and the late George were doing in the middle of a wilderness, but he knew better than to ask. They took him in and fed him and that was enough.

A couple of weeks after George died, Frank's body strength returned sufficiently and he felt it was time to move on, but to where, he wasn't certain. He deliberated about returning to Fort Lincoln, the burning question in his mind: was he wanted as a deserter? He was uncomfortable with that thought. George Custer and his brother Tom were harsh with the punishment of deserters, having executed some in past years.

Bill wasn't happy when Frank told him about his intention to leave but he gave him a shirt, pants, and an ill-fitting, worn coat that Frank's six-foot body fit into with difficulty. Attired and ready to go, Bill led him to a saddled horse, the mount that had belonged to the late George.

The two of them rode quietly down the trail, both men appreciating the quiet company. It was lonely in the wilderness. A few miles from the shack, they came to a fork in what appeared to be an old Indian trail.

"Give me an address and I'll send you the money for the horse when I get it," Frank said.

"You can go to Hell," Bill said. He turned his horse the other way and rode off without another word.[8]

Notes

[1]Finkel File, Oshkosh Public Museum, newspaper clippings of 1920, 1927, (probably) 1927 and a posthumous account by Finkel's second wife with dubious details deleted.

[2]Brininstool, E.A., *Troopers with Custer,* letter from Edward Godfrey to the author, May 21, 1921, reprinted on pages 247-248.

[3]*Ibid,* page 248.

[4]Finkel File, Oshkosh Public Museum. All important quotes are verbatim or close paraphrases. None are invented.

[5]*Ibid.*

[6]*Ibid.*

[7]*Ibid.* Finkel never understood why Bill didn't want a cross and puzzled over this for the next 50 years.

[8]*Ibid.*

Chapter Four

Before Little Big Horn

Frank Finkel was born on January 29, 1854 to Peter and Magdalene Finkle, the family name the census taker recorded in 1860.[1] His father was almost 20 years older than his mother, not unusual in Victorian times, when men were expected to be able to provide for their wives before they made respectable marriages.

He later remembered that his parents "had a reputation for uprightness and integrity which was a fine legacy for their descendents."[2] Peter Finckel, the original spelling, and Lena Windel, his wife, both came to the United States from the German states,[3] probably from Hanover, a section of Germany that had belonged to England until 1837, when the accession of Queen Victoria triggered a split. The Salic Law forbade a woman to rule unless the male line was extinct, and Victoria's "wicked uncle," the ultra-conservative Ernest Augustus, was very much alive when he took the throne in Hanover. He was followed by the tragic George VI, who lost one eye to a crust of stale bread in a food fight at an English boarding school and suffered the loss of the other eye to eyestrain and poor heredity.

"The blind King George" was the last King of Hanover and lost his throne when the Prussians won the Seven Weeks' War in 1866.

First Hanover became part of Prussia and later of Germany, and most Hanoverians who had emigrated during this turbulent period to the United States were very glad they did. The Finckels obviously were proud and grateful to be Americans—they gave all the male children Anglo-Saxon names—and they found their way to the American Midwest, a part of the growing United States that attracted many German immigrants.

Peter and Magdalene Finckel bought a farm in Union Township, Washington County, Ohio, in 1852, from Irish immigrants Philip and Ann McDermott for $90. in gold.[4] The McDermott's, according to the 1860 Census, owned another farm valued at $1400 and remained as neighbors of the Finckel's in the growing community of Irish and German immigrants.

Frank was born two years later in 1854. The Finckels were a hardy people and took to the soil, Peter Finckel throwing his heart, soul and body into it and, somehow, bringing from the Ohio earth enough corn, wheat, barley, and apples to get some return on his investment and to provide a minimal sustenance to his growing family. The 1860 Census recorded the farm's value being at $500, reflecting just a $410. increase over eight years.[5]

In addition to the wheat, barley, corn, and apples, Pete and Magdalene were also producing children; Henry, Peter, then Frank, followed by Charles and, with a pause of a few years, Adam and Joseph.[6] Magdalena must have wanted at least one daughter, so when Theresia showed up after 1860, she may have been satisfied and stopped bearing children.

The Finckels, like many immigrants of the time who went through name change or modification, gradually turned into the Finkels. They spoke German at home but their six sons and one daughter were sent to the common schools to learn their reading, writing and arithmetic in English along with the neighboring Irish and German children.

Frank, along with the other students learning to read and write, sat on benches, grouped by ability rather than age, and read their les-

The census of 1860

sons out loud, with the teacher, sometimes a teenager herself, walking from pupil to pupil listening to the recitations in what was called a "blab school." Frank grew up bilingual in English and German, literate, but not especially literary.

Farm work lasted from dawn to dusk and families sometimes discouraged their children from reading anything except the Bible on Sunday, and local newspapers whenever available. Reading in itself was deemed a waste of time, and nighttime reading, a waste of candles or whale oil, both expensive on a farmer's tight budget. Frank's reading skill, probably not of a high literary level, consequently developed from his reading of the local newspaper, like countless other frontier-bred Americans.

Hard work was the daily routine and with a plentitude of home-baked bread, whole milk and fresh vegetables and fruit, along with hearty soups of meat, vegetables and bones boiled for the marrow, strong bones and muscles were built.

Doctors were few and sickly children didn't live long. Life wasn't easy, and it wasn't expected to be any other way. The rustic Finkels, along with their German farming neighbors, spent little time at bookstores and beer gardens, unlike their urban kinsman in New York or Philadelphia. Social life was centered around the church, for the church-goers, and little else.

Plowing, scything the wheat and hay, picking apples, and taking care of the horses and cattle filled the daily schedule. One cousin though, Benjamin Franklin Finkel, proved that, despite the demands of farm life, learning was in the Finkel genetic system. He took time out from the farm work to study, entered the University of Chicago, and obtained a doctorate from the University of Pennsylvania. He taught in college, wrote several books and founded the *Mathematics Society of America Journal.*[7]

The Finkels were industrious and self-reliant, traits that Frank developed that would serve him well in the years ahead despite his limited education. When he was 15 years of age, life's demands would open the door for him to enter the school of life. His father, succumbing to the overly rigorous farm life, passed away at the age of 67. Perhaps it was the struggle to feed the family and quite possibly, the disappointment and heart wrench that goes with a battle that sees neither relief nor end.

Consequently, when Peter Finkel's worn body was buried in the Ohio soil, Frank at age 15 decided to leave the farm to find work. His brothers would stay home to farm for Lena and Theresia.

Money, Frank soon discovered, was precious for a young, relatively uneducated boy. It was hard earned. Initially shy at the outset but innately bright, Frank sought out work any way available. He was strong, and in farm life he had developed a knack for fixing things. He was able to work at odd jobs but barely earned enough to sustain his meager lifestyle. It was a difficult time to earn a living, virtually impossible to save for any kind of future which might include a marriage. Life on the open road, Frank discovered, had proven to be even more difficult than on the farm.

The era just after the Civil War was a difficult time for a relatively uneducated boy fresh from the farm to earn a living. It was a world on a tumultuous rush to a time that would be called the "The Gilded Age."

Civil service jobs became plums for people who "knew somebody"—but Finkel didn't "know anybody." Civil War officers who had become "gentlemen by act of Congress" struggled and pulled strings to wangle commissions in the tiny post-war Army so that they didn't have to work as shopkeepers or laborers. Senior officers scrambled for political appointments as revenue agents and tax collectors. Discharged enlistment men, North or South, were lucky to land a job working on the railroad. Laborers found it virtually impossible to save for any kind of future that might include a marriage.

The end of the 1860s and the beginning of the 1870s marked the beginning of the flight from the farm and changed American life forever. Railroads were linking the big cities and even the small towns in a way that the turnpikes and canals never could, and the need to finance the railroads led to the enormous growth of the New York Stock Exchange. The completion of the Transcontinental Railroad in the spring of 1869, as the Union Pacific met the Central Pacific in Utah and spanned the nation with tracks, touched off a spate of railroad building that reduced the isolation of inland cities and fostered enormous prosperity—at the top. Bankers, stock brokers and industrialists—the "robber barons"—became the new moneyed classes of America, gradually replacing the plantation overlords and large landowners who had been "the rich" during the early days of the Republic. Some of the railroad stock deals weren't entirely honest, and the freight rates angered farmers who needed to ship their crops to market. The gap between "rich" and "poor" began to widen and deepen. In 1868, the year Frank Finkel set out on his own, events were unfolding that would affect the rest of his life.

When Ulysses S. Grant was elected, his slogan as a victorious warrior was: "Let us have peace." He fostered the return of the former Confederate states as full-fledged members of the Union. But when the Ku Klux Klan murdered blacks and their white advocates, Grant fell on them like a thunderbolt with the Ku Klux Klan Act. Federal cavalrymen, including Custer, pursued marauding Klansmen all over the South, arresting 500 and sentencing 100 to Northern prisons. The Klan dissolved. The South began to assimilate back into the United States, though, in some cases, dark emotions would remain in place and be passed down to future generations.

Then a seminal series of events occurred that would impact and forever change Frank Finkel's life. President U.S. Grant fostered peace with the Indian tribes, notably the Sioux, who had fought the U.S. to a stalemate in Red Cloud's War of 1866–1868.

While Frank Finkel, by most definitions an itinerant journeyman, was knocking on doors in Iowa and Wisconsin hoping to find odd jobs particular to a handyman, the Gilded Age whirled with hype, exaggeration, fraud, fakery, quackery, and corruption. P.T. Barnum was at his best, promoting a planted, cement sculpture as a "petrified" ten-foot Indian "discovered" in Cardiff, New York; salesmen on the road were peddling cure-all patent medicines like Mexican Mustang Oil, electro-magnetic oil[8] and numerous snake oils guaranteed to remedy every ailment, something to cure everything for everyone. In Illinois, the state treasury was pillaged by political insiders through contracts with the penitentiary and the new state industrial university at Champaign.[9] Voters responded by demanding a new state constitution and in Washington, the Grant Administration was reeling from charges of corruption.

In January 27, 1872, Frank Finkel was in Chicago. How long he was there before that date is unknown but he surely saw the timbers of the wooden city that had been charred by the great fire that had raged and ravaged 17,500 buildings. How it effected his living quarters is also unknown, but he had made a decision upon which he would act that day. His living quarters would not be a matter of question.

Unknown to him, events had occurred that would re-direct his road of life, a road that would ultimatcly, and inadvertently, take him to a life in a far-away place, probably far exceeding his hopes and wishes.

In March of 1869 in Washington D.C., President Grant appointed a close friend, Maj. Gen. John Rawlins, as Secretary of War. Rawlins was tubercular and died of the disease just six months later. Grant's subsequent appointments of William Worth Belknap as Secretary of War and Columbus Delano as Secretary of the Interior resulted in the establishment by the Secretaries of corrupt business enterprises at the Army posts and at the Indian agencies. Excessive profiteering became the norm, exploiting the Indians and soldiers who were forced to purchase inferior and over-priced goods at the Post Trader or the Agency store, both protected monopolies with licenses doled out as political patronage. The practice set in motion a rippling anger and discontent by the Indians, who were forced to accept rancid bacon and rock-hard flour as staple items. It would create a desperation that would force some to leave their agencies for the old way of life to avoid starvation a few years down the road, with consequences Frank Finkel would experience as the central event of his life.

Notes

[1]U.S. Census of 1860.

[2]Finkel File, Oshkosh Public Museum, unpublished book on the history of southwestern Washington. Note that the names and birth order of the first five children of Peter and Magdalena Finkle, including Frank, match perfectly between the 1860 Census and the 1905 article. Joseph apparently hadn't been baptized and Theresia hadn't yet been born in 1860.

[3]U.S. Census of 1860.

[4]Deed transfer, Phillip McDermott to Peter Finkle, Ohio State Historical Society.

[5]U.S. Census of 1860.

[6]*Ibid.*

[7]*Who Was Who in America,* 1943-1950 edition only, "Finkel, Benjamin Franklin," page 186.

[8]Young, Harvey, *The Toadstool Millionaires: A Social History of Patent Medicines in America before Federal Regulation,* Chapter 11.

[9]Cronon, William, *Nature's Metropolis: Chicago and the Great West.* New York: W. W. Norton and Co., 1991.

Chapter Five

Enlisting and Everything Prussian

Saturday, January 27, 1872, was a crisp, cold day in Chicago.[1] It was a typical day for that month, the average temperature was 12 degrees below zero[2] and Frank Finkel decided to act on a decision. He would enlist in the United States Army. He also had an idea.

The American-born Regular Army men, from the Old Army when officers were addressed in the third person and enlisted men never spoke until they were spoken to, had a wry joke about peacetime enlistments: a soldier is a man who's too proud to beg, too dumb to steal, and too lazy to work. Foreign-born recruits, however, frequently signed up, many because of language problems. The Irish immigrants had suffered because of an inadequate education system in Ireland that the British Parliament had difficulty financing[3] and the Germans, Italians, and Danes had problems both in reading and in speaking English. The Army was a great place to practice spoken English for five years. Three meals a day and a bed were added incentives.

Many officers of the 1870s were adventurers who had served in the Civil War or in European armies. Many enlisted men could

be characterized as soldiers of misfortune. Few, if any, had any desire
to kill Indians. The Sioux Treaty of 1868 and Custer's defeat of the
Southern Plains tribes at the end of the decade had already ended the
serious Indian fighting in the West—or so it was thought.

When Frank Finkel sat down to put his name on the United
States Army enlistment papers, on that cold day in 1872, he undoubtedly had a good sense of self-esteem because of his German
ancestry. Things German were held in high respect by the American
people. Teutonic culture was viewed through a rose-colored lens and
understandably so. Germany was a land of great cultural achiev-
ers, a veritable land of enlightened scientists, thinkers, composers
and writers. It was home to musical giants: the Bachs, Beethoven,
Wagner; German-Austrians Mozart, Schubert, and the Strauss family, all reaching great heights with symphonies, operas, and concer-
tos; philosophers Kant and Hegel with thought development; scientists Alexander von Humboldt with biological geographies, Rudolf
Virchow fathering pathology and public health; writers: Goethe,
whose Magnum Opus *Faust* became a world-class literary treasure,
Schiller, poet and playwright, author of "Wilhelm Tell," and Heinrich
Heine, the lyric poet so often set to music by Robert Schumann and
other composers. Germany was a land which prominent American
authors such as Washington Irving, Longfellow, Fenimore Cooper,
Bayard Taylor and a host of others visited for inspiration and intel-
lectual sustenance. William James studied medicine in Germany just
after the Civil War. American admiration for German culture was
great. And as the years passed, in America, it widened in other areas
as well.[4]

During the American Civil War, German immigrants, aboli-
tionist almost to the last man and strong advocates of preserving the
Union, had flooded into the Union Army. Charles Godfrey Leland,
an Anglo-Saxon who understood German and was credited with
changing the term "abolition" to "emancipation," invented the most
beloved comic figure of the decade—Hans Breitmann, the bump-
tious German-American who described his amusing exploits in
smooth verse and broken English. Lincoln kept a well-thumbed copy
of Hans Breitmann poems in the White House.[5] Henry Clay Work,
greatest writer of American popular song after the death of Stephen

Courtesy of the Department of the Army

Prussian influenced dress uniforms replaced the French influence in 1871.

Foster, invented "Corporal Schnapps," a soldier of the Union who talked like Hans Breitmann—*Ach, mein Fraeulein,* you *bist* so very unkind"—but fought "to keep *mein* country free." Having settled largely in northern farming states, the German contribution to the army of Abraham Lincoln was quite significant—180,000 Germans served in Lincoln's army, more than any other foreign-born component—even slightly more than the Irish with 175,000.

Prior to the war that ended with the unification of the several German states into the one nation of Germany, "Germany" had been a collection of independent states, and Prussia was the largest and the

A Black regiment in their Prussian-style dress uniforms.

most visible state in northern Germany. The Prussians maintained an army famous since before the Prussian "Baron" Friedrich von Steuben reorganized George Washington's Continentals at Valley Forge.

Dating from the heyday of Louis XIV and Napoleon Bonaparte, France, at the time, was viewed as the bully-boy of Europe, having precipitated war with the Germanic states, and just about every-one else, on numerous occasions. Indeed, the wide-ranging armies of Bonaparte poured over Europe from the Atlantic to Russia, only to be stopped by the winter snows. Little sympathy was given to Napoleon III of France, who had developed the habit of throwing his county's weight around, especially after he violated the Monroe Doctrine by invading Mexico while the United States was locked in the Civil War.[6]

Perception is one thing though, and reality often something entirely different. The Franco-Prussian War was, reportedly, the last of three European wars machinated by Bismarck to unite the Germanic states in January of 1871. However, the world-view, the English-speaking view, was sympathetic to Prussia and the confed-eration of Teutonic states. Sympathy for the Prussians was spurred by prominent British authors such as Thomas Carlyle and Edward Creasy and "Oxford School" historian Edward A. Freeman, whose sentiment was that in the Franco-Prussian War it was the "high mission" of Germany to bring an end to the French "conspiracy" against world peace. The fact that Crown Princess Victoria of Prussia was the eldest daughter of Queen Victoria and that her son, Prince Wilhelm, was Queen Victoria's favorite grandson was also crucial in England.[7]

The American public took much of its cue from England. The *London Times* was then the most influential newspaper in the English-speaking world and its influence on American newspapers was profound. British sympathy to Prussia was natural because France was Britain's traditional enemy, and that sympathy was conveyed by the *Times* to newspapers in the United States who picked up on it and passed it on to a nation growing up reading newspapers. When the confederation of German states, the pastoral, Grimm's-fairytale-like cultural repository, methodically put a military machine together that quickly humiliated the French, it was viewed with considerable admiration, if not awe—Germany had risen from *Das Land der Dichter und Denker*—a collage of writers, poets, philosophers and composers—to become the upstart military power of Europe in a single decade.[8]

Admiration often gives birth to imitation and the American military proved to be no exception. In the United States the War Department, impressed with the swift Prussian military skills demonstrated so ably against the ever-powerful French, was quick to adopt the Prussian spiked helmet as its regular dress headgear, an indication of the high regard the American soldier had for the Prussian. The U.S. Cavalry and Artillery and the Signal Corps received their spiked helmets in 1871, while Finkel was still a hungry vagabond in Chicago. Frank Finkel recognized this perspective—Prussia was the place to come from if you wanted the Army to admire you. He saw opportunity. His German ethnicity and his fluent German, with the sharp North German accent of Prussia or Hanover, could be put to good use.

When Frank Finkel sat down with Captain G. F. M. Young of the 7th Cavalry to join up, being a resourceful young man, he had to know something about the Army. He was surely aware that the pay scale gave a private a monthly earning of $15.00 and a sergeant

Courtesy of the Little Bighorn Battlefield Memorial Museum

Sargeant Jeremiah Finley of the 7th Cavalry and his horse Carlo at Fort Rice in 1875, in his Prussian-style dress uniform.

$40.00. It was a significant difference. His thrifty, dollar-conscious mind had to click into that difference.

Finkel, the bilingual German-American farm boy, born in Ohio, who had learned his way in the world in the Gilded Age, reached for the Captain's pen to put that education to use.

When he signed up, he gave his name as "August Finckle," reverting to the second, and still heavily Germanic spelling of the family name, originally "Finckel." He gave his birthplace as "Berlin, Prussia," and probably to capitalize on Prussia's tremendous military reputation after the Franco-Prussian War, he gave his age as 27 so he could pose as a veteran, thus hoping to hasten an advance in rank.

He later told Charles Windolph, his best friend in the Army, that he had been a Prussian officer, and Windolph, who was born in Bergen, Hanover, not an intrinsic Prussian state, believed him—even though in a country given to the class system, a Prussian officer,

Sample of Prussian script from a contemporary primer published in Berlin.

whether of the aristocracy or the educated gentry, would not have joined another Army as an enlisted man.

But the recruiting officer, delighted to have a new recruit, did not question him. It is not noted either, that a inquiry relative to Frank's experience was posed by the Army recruiter. The recruiting officer, Captain G. F. M. Young of the 8th Cavalry recorded "August Finckle's" height as 6 feet, 1/2 inch, his eyes as "grey," his hair as "dark" and his complexion as "dark." His tall, sturdy physique and his lifelong farmer's tan may actually have made him look like a man in his middle 20s.

Finkel's legally required signatures on the recruiting form—he signed twice—reveal, however, that he was no Prussian: the hand script is the rolling penmanship of the American common schools, with some mild German influence only on the capital F in the family name. Prussian script slants sharply from right top to left bottom and the letters are formed so differently from American script that the Prussian handscript is illegible to Anglo-Americans.

The signature that Finkel had signed himself into the U.S. Army with would be a key element in identifying him as the lone survivor of Custer's Last Stand.

Notes
[1]Diary of James Harvey Rhea, 1872 Morgan County, IL.

[2]Cox, Henry Joseph Armington, *John Howard-The weather and climate of Chicago*, Google.

[3]House of Commons, 12 June 1840.

[4]Gazley, John, *American Opinion of German Unification, 1848-1871*, Columbia University, 1926.

[5]Leland, Charles Godfrey, in *American National Biography*, Volume 13, pages 462-463, *Dictionary Of American Biography*, Volume 6, pages 158-160, *The National Cyclopaedia Of American Biography*, Volume 5, page 356.

[6]Greusel, John, *Blood and Iron: Origin of German Empire as Revealed by Character of Its Founder, Bismarck*.

Howard, Michael, *Franco-Prussian War: The German Invasion of France 1870-1871*, Revised Edition.

[7]*Ibid.*

[8]*Ibid.*

THE UNITED STATES OF AMERICA.

OATH OF ENLISTMENT AND ALLEGIANCE.

State of *Illinois* } ss:
Town of *Chicago*

I, *August Finckle* , born in *Berlin* , in
the State of *Prussia* , and by occupation a *Clerk*
DO HEREBY ACKNOWLEDGE to have voluntarily enlisted this *Twenty Seventh* day
of *January* , 187*2*, as a *Soldier* in the Army of the United States of America,
for the period of FIVE YEARS, unless sooner discharged by proper authority: And do also agree to
accept from the United States such bounty, pay, rations, and clothing as are or may be established by
law. And I do solemnly swear, that I am *Twenty Seven* years and *c*
months of age, and know of no impediment to my serving honestly and faithfully as a Soldier for five
years under this enlistment contract with the United States. And I, *August Finckle*
do also solemnly swear, that I will bear true faith and allegiance to the **United States of America**,
and that I will serve them honestly and faithfully against all their enemies or opposers whomsoever; and
that I will observe and obey the orders of the President of the United States, and the orders of the officers
appointed over me, according to the Rules and Articles of War.

August Finckle (SEAL)

Subscribed and duly sworn to before me, this *27th* day of *January*, A. D. 187*2*

S.B. Wÿnning,
Captain 8 Cavalry
Recruiting Officer.

I CERTIFY, ON HONOR, That I have carefully examined the above-named recruit, agreeably to the General Regulations of the Army, and
that, in my opinion, he is free from all bodily defects and mental infirmity which would, in any way, disqualify him from performing the duties of a
soldier.

S.B. Wÿnning
Capt 8th U.S. Cavalry
Examining Officer.

I CERTIFY, ON HONOR, That I have minutely inspected the above-named recruit *August Finckle* , previously
to his enlistment, and that he was entirely sober when enlisted; that, to the best of my judgment and belief, he is of lawful age; and that I have
accepted and enlisted him into the service of the United States under this contract of enlistment as duly qualified to perform the duties of an able-
bodied soldier, and, in doing so, have strictly observed the Regulations which govern the Recruiting Service. This soldier has *grey* eyes,
dark hair, *dark* complexion, is *6* feet *½* inches high.

S.B. Wÿnning (SEAL)
Captain 8 Cavalry
Recruiting Officer, United States Army.

[A. G. O. No. 73.]

Frank's Enlistment Papers

46

No. _____

August Finckle

Enlisted at *Chicago Ill* on

the *27th* day of *January* 187*2*,

by *Capt R S M Young*

8th Regiment of *Cavalry*

_____ enlistment; last served in Company (   )

_____ Reg't of _____

Discharged _____ , 18 _____

DIRECTIONS.

Enlistments must, in all cases, be taken in triplicate. The recruiting officer will send one copy to the Adjutant General with his monthly accounts, a second to the superintendent with his monthly return, and a third to the depot at the time the recruits are sent there. In cases of soldiers re-enlisted in a regiment, or of regimental recruits, the third copy of the enlistment will be sent at its date to regimental headquarters for file.

Received A. G. O. _____

Assigned to the _____ Regiment

of _____ , U. S. Army.

DECLARATION OF RECRUIT.

I, *August Finckle*, DO DECLARE, That I have neither wife nor child; that I have never been discharged from the United States Service on account of disability, or by sentence of a court martial, or by order before the expiration of term of enlistment; and that I am of the legal age to enlist of my own accord, and believe myself to be physically qualified to perform the duties of an able-bodied soldier.

desiring to ENLIST in the Army of the United States, for the term of FIVE YEARS.

GIVEN at *Chicago Illinois* this *27th* day of *January*, 187*2*.

August H Finckle

WITNESS:

Frank's Enlistment Papers

Chapter Six

Life After Little Big Horn

Sergeant Finkel remembered that he rode about two days through the Montana wilderness before he found a boom town in the middle of "next to nowhere," tucked on the bank of the Missouri River. The principal port of call for river steamboats was Fort Benton, then the largest inland steamboat harbor west of St. Louis. It was a rip-roaring river town where Missouri River steamboats unloaded their cargos onto "bull trains," convoys of wagons pulled by teams of oxen which would lug the loads of cargo to destinations on the many roads leading from Fort Benton that expanded out like the spokes of a wheel.

Fort Benton had originally been a fur-trading post operated by hardy frontier Scots and French-Canadians, often with Indian wives as interpreters, but later it became the steamboat hub of the West. During the Montana Gold Rush of 1866, Fort Benton had shipped two-and-a-half tons of gold dust downriver to St. Louis. There were more than a dozen saloons in Fort Benton, and it was a great place for a man on the run to hide or, for a man with a secret to lose himself.[1]

American Fur Company trading post at Fort Benton in 1860.

When Finkel arrived at Fort Benton, he discovered that the Army had withdrawn from the post. As he was becoming acquainted with the town, he picked up an old copy of the *Bismarck Tribune* and discovered that his entire company had been wiped out at the Little Big Horn. He was thunderstruck.[2] Like Benteen and Reno atop Reno Hill, he may have expected Custer to defeat the Sioux and Cheyenne in the end, and he must have been stunned, not to mention grief-stricken, to find out how many of his friends were dead. His own name appeared, fourth from the bottom on the front page of the *Bismarck Tribune* under George and Tom Custer, Sergeant Bobo, and Sergeant Finley. His emotions had to be in some state of turmoil upon such news. The death of everyone in the five companies, Custer included, must have taken some time to absorb.

He may have had some misgivings about his own survival but there must have been some confusion in his mind: he supposedly told his second wife, long after his survival of the Little Big Horn battle was public knowledge, that he tried to claim a discharge from the Army, but was unable to prove he'd been a soldier without two witnesses.[3] On the surface, it resonates like a cover-up for his successful escape being construed as desertion in the face of the enemy. It could not have rested easily with him and apparently, it did not, for it would be 44 years before he could share his story with others. It would be a secret he would keep with difficulty.

FIRST ACCOUNT OF THE CUSTER MASSACRE.

TRIBUNE EXTRA.

Price 25 Cents.   BISMARCK, D. T., JULY 6, 1876.

MASSACRED

GEN. CUSTER AND 261 MEN THE VICTIMS.

NO OFFICER OR MAN OF 5 COMPANIES LEFT TO TELL THE TALE.

3 Days Desperate Fighting by Maj. Reno and the Remainder of the Seventh.

Full Details of the Battle.

LIST OF KILLED AND WOUNDED.

THE BISMARCK TRIBUNE'S SPECIAL CORRESPONDENT SLAIN.

Squaws Mutilate and Rob the Dead

Victims Captured Alive Tortured in a Most Fiendish Manner.

What Will Congress Do About It?

Shall This Be the Beginning of the End?

The Bismarck Tribune *story that Frank read in Fort Benton*

Fort Benton steamboat levee with piles of freight waiting for overland freighting.

Leery with his status as a "deserter" and thoughts of the Custer executions in 1866 ever in mind, Finkel stowed away on a river steamer on the Yellowstone River after he quietly left Fort Benton. He slipped aboard as the boat touched the riverbank to pick up wood, after the captain turned him down as a crew member because he still looked too feeble to be worth his fare.

Before long, Finkel was caught and turned in to the Captain of the boat. He offered to work off his passage by helping to repair things that needed fixing. He had skills pertinent to the situation: a social skill that enabled him to relate to people and rudimentary carpentry skills developed on the family farm. When the riverboat hit a snag on the river, opportunity opened up for Frank Finkel.

River steamboats on the Missouri, belching smoke by day and lit up by night, were a common sight in the 1870s, before the railroads connected the towns along the river to Chicago and other hubs of transportation.

At any given time there might have been 40 working freight boats carrying passengers and mail, touching Fort Benton and then heading south for St. Louis. The "Mountain Boats," as they were

Jerkline Mule Train in front of T. C. Power store in Fort Benton, 1870s.

called, were specially designed for the wild Missouri, with spoon-bill shaped bows and flat bottoms that could navigate in as little as 20 inches of water. The boats had to be shallow draft because the depth of the river shifted unpredictably due to sandbars and run-off from the land. Two spars on the front of the cargo deck could be lowered to attach the boat to rocks on the riverbank and help haul the boats over sandbars with chains and capstans, and an extra boost from the engine. The boatmen called this "grasshoppering."

The Mountain Boats were broad of beam, usually about 30 feet, and generally about 180 feet long, though some were much longer. The steamboats were always stern-wheelers, driven ahead by one paddle at the fantail of the boat. Sidewheels were traditional on the lower Mississippi and on ocean-going ships, before the screw propeller became general about this time. But the twin sidewheels often hit floating logs and became shattered or jammed. Even the stern-wheels were vulnerable on the turbulent Missouri and accounted for a number of breakdowns. More dreaded were boiler explosions, which sometimes killed or scalded the stokers working on the engines. Stokers on Mountain Boats, in fact, worked short shifts, only a few hours at a time, so they'd have the strength and energy to fight internal fires.[4]

Good captains made good money and some of them were legendary: Grant Marsh, "King of the Rivermen," had hauled the wounded survivors of Reno Hill 710 miles in only 54 hours in the aftermath of the Little Big Horn catastrophe. Usually, the Mountain Boats hauled freight and passengers at a more leisurely speed.

Squatters, settlers living on unregistered land, made pocket money cutting wood for the boats that they piled at landings along the riverbanks, and they sometimes sold game to the crews. The boilers and the sternwheels gave the captains a lot of headaches, but it was collisions that sank most of the boats. Once the railroads took a lot of the risk out of travel, the Mountain Boats vanished almost overnight. By the end of the 1880s, they were history and Fort Benton, their raucous port of call, became a sleepy town serving local farmers and hunters, no longer the biggest inland seaport between St. Louis and San Francisco.

Frank Finkel was able to patch things up after the boat became damaged on a snag and kept it moving. The riverboat captain offered him a regular job, but Finkel backed off, claiming he was thinking of trying to get a medical discharge from the Army so he could pursue another line of work.[5] It is noteworthy that Frank, at that time, was burying his secret. It could indicate that he had made a decision to desert the Army, probably with a growing fear of being branded a deserter in the face of the enemy.

In retrospect, showing up in a sergeant's blouse with a bullet hole in the shoulder and the body of his horse found dead at the confluence of the Rosebud and Yellowstone Rivers should have been sufficient proof to establish legitimacy to his story. Perhaps. But returning to Fort Abraham Lincoln to report could have been a costly thing. The public excitement and near-hysteria at the out-come of the battle created an atmosphere in which political blame was being tossed about and the arrival of an enlisted man who "ran away" from the scene could have been a convenient diversion. The outcome for Finkel was filled with uncertain and unpleasant possibilities. An

River Steamboat.

intelligent man, he had to think of those unpleasant possibilities. He chose to go in a direction opposite of Fort Abraham Lincoln.

He got on the next steamboat and headed south, away from the Army and Fort Abraham Lincoln. St. Louis, founded by German settlers brought in by the French in the days of the Louisiana Territory, was then perhaps the most German city in America. Joseph Pulitzer got his start there at a German-language newspaper, the *Westliche Post*, before he bought up the *St. Louis Post Dispatch* and later headed for New York. Finkel, of German ethnicity, had to feel comfortable in St. Louis so he stayed there, working for a dairy company delivering milk on horse-drawn wagons. Farm-raised, with cavalry experience and the administrative experience as Second Sergeant of C Company, he could only have been a prize employee with his knowledge of the horses that delivered the milk, the cows that produced it, and the paperwork that pulled the business together. He became adept at the dairy business and even saved some money beyond his room and board. He would use it to go west. He wanted to see California.

Finkel had a yearning to see the Golden Gate. He may have been attracted to the area for its esthetics: the harbor, the windswept beaches, wildlife corridors, oak woodlands and redwood forests, but more likely the farmland. He sensed that there might be opportunity there since it was opening up to large-scale settlement due to the completion of the Transcontinental Railroad.

Joining the spirit of the time, he took the train to cover the 2073 mile span between the two cities. When he arrived there he savored the mellow climate, but California was too dry for the kind of farming he was familiar with and wanted to pursue. And the land was already too expensive for his thrifty nature.

He turned north to what had once been Oregon Territory, the beckoning lure of the Pacific Coast when California still belonged to Mexico before the Gold Rush and the Mexican War.

Finkel took the stagecoach, riding on top of thick leather straps and behind six horses because the railroad had not yet stretched that far. He soon discovered Dayton, Washington, a small town on the Idaho border, tucked in the Walla Walla Valley and at the confluence of the Touchet River and Patit Creek. The rich smell of good farmland told him he was where he wanted to be. The railroad had not yet arrived, but it was coming, and Finkel knew, too, that once it did, Dayton would be a town with a future.

Named after a settler, Jesse Day, Dayton had first been settled in 1859, and wheat farming had begun to replace grazing just two years later. Finkel grew up with wheat farming in Ohio, and the soil and the air felt right for apples, another crop he knew well. The town had been platted and named and a post office had been established in 1872. There were lots of Germans too, just like St. Louis.[6] He was in his comfort zone.

A German immigrant named Jacob Weinhard established the Weinhard Brewery when he realized that the soil and climate were excellent for barley as well as wheat. The horse-drawn stagecoach served the town while Dayton waited for the railroad. When Finkel arrived, Dayton was still "rough around the edges," a lumberjack's and miner's town with a brothel listed among its other businesses. But "respectable" family people were growing in number, and the farming was good for some of the crops Finkel understood. Best of all, it wasn't as hot as Montana and the Dakotas in the summer, or as bitter cold in the winter.

Finkel's carpentry skills were soon to be developed for more than makeshift coffins and steamboat repairs. A large-scale fire wiped out some of the seedier buildings about the time that the Oregon Railroad and Navigation Company finished its depot in 1881 and as Dayton rebuilt itself, it started to grow, almost exponentially, with Finkel sawing and fitting when he wasn't planting and harvesting for established farms. Shipping crops by railroad and the hard work of industrious Anglo-Saxons and of German-Americans like Jacob Weinhard and Frank Finkel turned Dayton into a respectable and prosperous community through the 1880s and 1890s.

About the time Finkel arrived, Joseph Wolfstein started the trend toward upscale homes with a one-story Greek Revival home built in 1880. John Brining bought the Greek Revival house from Wolfstein in 1883 and constructed a two-story addition in the Queen Anne style. Houses in ornate styles like the Italianate, the Queen Anne, and even the flamboyant Gothic Revival style that emulated the Middle Ages, began to replace those clapboard buildings with their saloon facades that had survived the fire. Dayton was upscaling.

There was a lot of carpenter's work in those Gothic Revivals, and Frank Finkel seized the opportunity. Carpentry paid well. In a week he could earn $40.00, a sergeant's pay for a month in the Army.

There was something else Finkel liked about Dayton, a girl named Delia Rainwater. Delia was said to be part Cherokee. This was a serious concern in Victorian times. James Butler Hickok is said to have left his family and headed West to become Wild Bill Hickok when his mother and father refused to let him marry a girl who was one-eighth Shawnee. Frontier legend and lore held deep-seated prejudices that "Injun blood" would somehow produce skulking, scalping-hunting murderers. As a result, Delia's suitors were fewer in number than an attractive girl such as she was would have normally attracted. But it proved to be no bother to Frank Finkel. The ignorance that fosters prejudice was not his. He knew Indians. He shrugged off Delia's rumored Cherokee blood and went calling.

Jacob Rainwater's first wife, Catherine Lucinda Williamson, died "around" 1880 after bearing Delia and eight other children. About four years later, in 1884, Jacob re-married. His second wife was Nellie Pintler, a German girl. Jacob, eventually and remarkably, fathered nine more children.

First Land Transaction

When Frank reached for Delia's hand, she graciously handed it to him. He was engaged to be married. The wedding would be in January. Preparations had to be made, and not only for the wedding. Delia's father would make those arrangements but Frank would have to make arrangements for a home for his bride. His living quarters would not be at all suitable. He was a boarder, living at the farm of a neighboring farmer, Charlie Grupe.

In December 1885, he embarked on the realization of his desire as a young man, to have his own farm. It would become a matter of record on December 14, 1885, when he purchased it for $500.00 in gold. One month later he would bring his 18-year-old bride, daughter of the successful Jake Rainwater, to their new home. The house was a few miles from the center of town. It was also a world away from the valley of the Little Big Horn River.

Jacob Rainwater

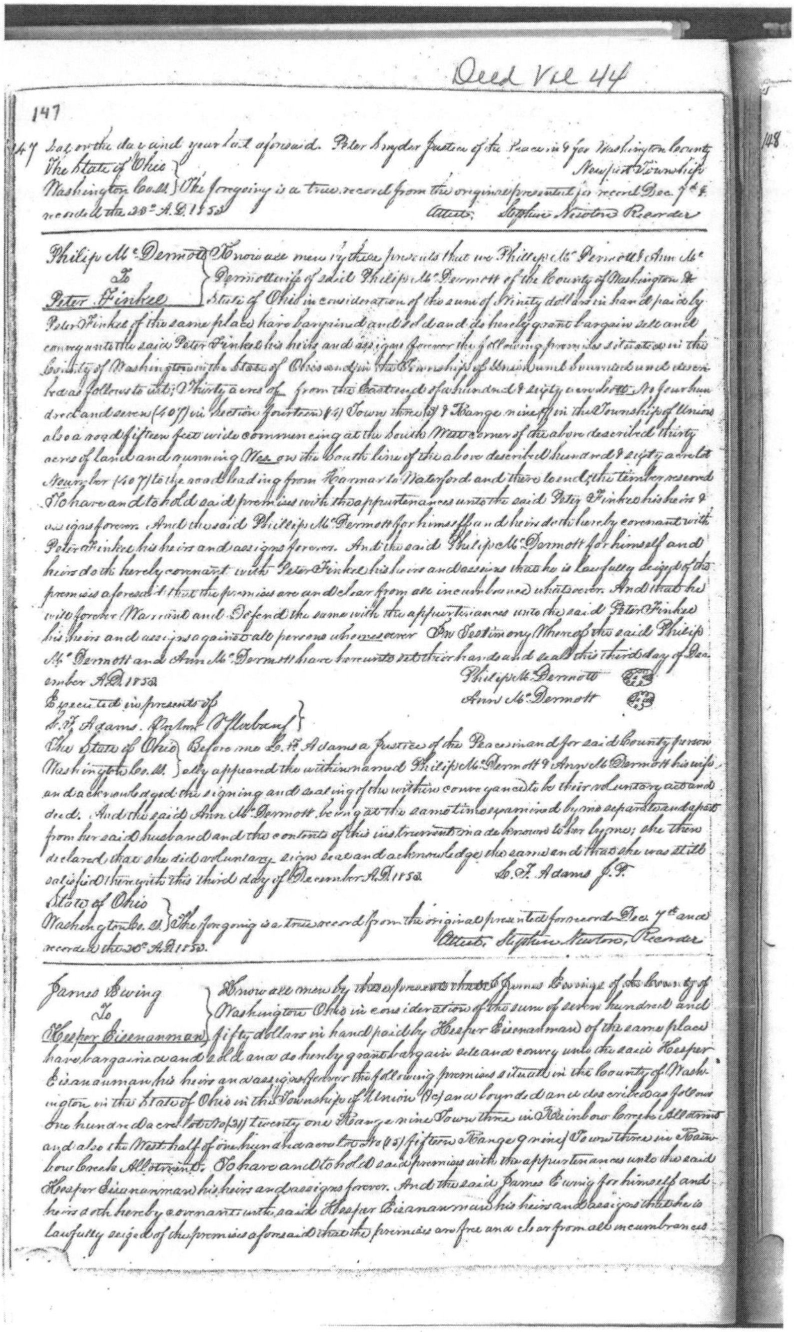
Deed Vol 44

147

147 Sal on the day and year last aforesaid. Peter Snyder Justice of the Peace in & for Washington County
The State of Ohio } Newport Township
Washington Co. ss } The foregoing is a true record from the original presented for record Dec. 7th &
recorded the 20th A.D. 1852 Attest: Stephen Newton Recorder

Philip McDermott To Peter Finkee } Know all men by these presents that we Phillip McDermott & Ann McDermott wife of said Philip McDermott of the County of Washington & State of Ohio in consideration of the sum of Ninety dollars in hand paid by Peter Finkee of the same place have bargained and sold and do hereby grant bargain sell and convey unto the said Peter Finkee his heirs and assigns forever the following premises situate in the County of Washington in the State of Ohio and in the Township of Union and bounded and described as follows to wit; Thirty acres of from the East end of a hundred & sixty acre lott No four hundred and seven (407) in Section fourteen (14) Town three (3) & Range nine (9) in the Township of Union also a road fifteen feet wide commencing at the South West corner of the above described thirty acres of land and running West on the South line of the above described hundred & sixty acre lot Number (407) to the road leading from Harmar to Waterford and there to end; the timber reserved. To have and to hold said premises with the appurtenances unto the said Peter Finkee his heirs & assigns forever. And the said Phillip McDermott for himself and heirs doth hereby covenant with Peter Finkee his heirs and assigns forever. And the said Philip McDermott for himself and heirs doth hereby covenant with Peter Finkee his heirs and assigns that he is lawfully seized of the premises aforesaid that the premises are and clear from all incumbrances whatsoever. And that he will forever Warrant and Defend the same with the appurtenances unto the said Peter Finkee his heirs and assigns against all persons whomsoever. In Testimony Whereof the said Philip McDermott and Ann McDermott have hereunto set their hands and seal this third day of December A.D. 1852
Philip McDermott (Seal)
Ann McDermott (Seal)
Executed in presents of
L. F. Adams. [illegible]
The State of Ohio } Before me L. F. Adams a Justice of the Peace in and for said County person-
Washington Co. ss } ally appeared the within named Philip McDermott & Ann McDermott his wife and acknowledged the signing and sealing of the within conveyance to be their voluntary act and deed. And the said Ann McDermott being at the same time examined by me separate and apart from her said husband and the contents of this instrument made known to her by me; she then declared that she did voluntary sign seal and acknowledge the same and that she was still satisfied therewith this third day of December A.D. 1852. L. F. Adams J.P.
State of Ohio }
Washington Co. ss } The foregoing is a true record from the original presented for record Dec. 7th and recorded the 20th A.D. 1852. Attest: Stephen Newton, Recorder

James Ewing To Hesper Eisenanman } Know all men by these presents that I James Ewing of the County of Washington Ohio in consideration of the sum of seven hundred and fifty dollars in hand paid by Hesper Eisenanman of the same place have bargained and sold and do hereby grant bargain sell and convey unto the said Hesper Eisenanman his heirs and assigns forever the following premises situate in the County of Washington in the State of Ohio in the Township of Union (&c) and bounded and described as follows One hundred acre lot No (21) twenty one Range nine Town three in Rainbow Creek Allotment and also the West half of one hundred acre lot No (15) fifteen Range 9 nine Town three in Rainbow Creek Allotment. To have and to hold said premises with the appurtenances unto the said Hesper Eisenanman his heirs and assigns forever. And the said James Ewing for himself and heirs doth hereby covenant with said Hesper Eisenanman his heirs and assigns that he is lawfully seized of the premises aforesaid that the premises are free and clear from all incumbrances

The deed for the first land transaction

Courtesy of Naedene Shearer, Columbia County Courthouse

On January 23, 1886, 39 days after his first land purchase, Frank Finkel took the hand of 18-year-old Delia Rainwater in matrimony; it was about five months short of the 10th anniversary of the Little Big Horn. He had never spoken of the battle at the Little Big Horn, nor of his service in the U.S. Army, to anyone in Dayton. His secret had been kept.

Signing the Marriage Certificate

The wedding took place at the house of J.L. Hunt. Finkel signed the marriage certificate book as "Finckle" but the clerk signed the actual marriage license as "Finkle." Delia gave her birthplace as Oregon. Finkel, perhaps, still looking over his shoulder, left his birthplace blank.[7]

On their wedding night, Finkel's teenaged bride asked her 32-year-old husband about the old gunshot wound on his left side and

The marriage certificate

Courtesy Milton Koch

Frank Finkel in the late 1800s

the other scar on his leg. Holding to his secret, perhaps, fearful that his new life could come to a crashing end, he told her he'd been shot in a fight with some Indians. He didn't say where the fight took place. [8] The bullet in his side eventually worked its way to the surface many years later, just above the navel, causing a nasty abscess, and Frank and Delia had a surgeon take it out. The wound healed cleanly.

On a document now at the Columbia County Courthouse auditor's office in Dayton, the clerk recording the land transactions actually spelled Frank's name both ways—Finkle and Finkel.[9] Frank Finkel himself didn't sign. A lot of people in the 19th century, farmers especially, didn't know how to read and the clerk who recorded the deed signed the papers. Even when the farmer could read and write, as Finkel could, this was standard operating procedure. The family surname spelling continued to fluctuate through the 1890s, as Frank bought or sold 10 farms and two more houses and the clerks kept signing the deeds. The lot numbers and Delia's name on the deeds indicate that he was the same person, despite the shift in spelling.

Frank Finkel, working even harder now that he was a husband and part of a respectable family, used his sparse money and his skills in carpentry and farming to speculate in land, building thriving farms, then selling some of them and buying more vacant land. He also took advantage of the Homestead Act of 1862 and claimed at

THE UNITED STATES OF AMERICA.

Homestead Certificate No. *2295*
Application *3867* } ss.   To all to Whom these Presents shall Come---GREETING:

WHEREAS, There has been deposited in the General Land Office of the United States a Certificate of the Register of the Land Office at *Walla Walla, Washington* whereby it appears that, pursuant to the Act of Congress approved 20th May, 1862, "To Secure Homesteads to Actual Settlers on the Public Domain," and the acts supplemental thereto, the claim of *Frank Finkel* has been established and duly consummated, in conformity to law, for the

East half of the South East quarter of the North west quarter of the South East quarter of Section Nine, in Township Nine North of Range Thirty Nine East of the Willamette meridian in Washington containing one hundred and twenty acres

according to the Official Plat of the Survey of the said Land, returned to the General Land Office by the Surveyor General.

NOW, KNOW YE, That there is, therefore, granted by the United States unto the said *Frank Finkel,* the tract of land above described:

TO HAVE AND TO HOLD the said tract of Land, with the appurtenances thereof, unto the said *Frank Finkel* and to *his* his heirs and assigns forever, subject to any vested and accrued water rights for mining, agricultural, manufacturing or other purposes, and rights to ditches and reservoirs used in connection with such water rights, as may be recognized and acknowledged by the local customs, laws and decisions of Courts, and also subject to the right of the proprietor of a vein or lode, to extract and remove his ore therefrom, should the same be found to penetrate or intersect the premises hereby granted, as provided by law.

IN TESTIMONY WHEREOF, I, *Benjamin Harrison* President of the United States of America, have caused these letters to be made Patent, and the Seal of the General Land Office to be hereunto affixed.

Given under my hand, at the City of Washington, the *Thirtieth* day of *June,* in the year of our Lord one thousand eight hundred and *ninety-Two,* and of the Independence of the United States the one hundred and *Sixteenth.*

BY THE PRESIDENT: *Benjamin Harrison*

By *M. McKean* Secretary.

S. P. Roberts Recorder of the General Land Office.

Recorded Vol. *5* Page *215*

Filed for Record at *1:30* o'clock *P.* M., *October 14* A. D. 189*8* and recorded at the request of *Frank Finkel*

By _____ Deputy.   *Harper,* *County Auditor*

The Homestead Land claim, signed by the clerk, not Frank

least one 160-acre tract for a simple registration fee and improved and sold it. As documents with his name were being officially filed, he must have spent the first few years looking over his shoulder. The citizens in Dayton grew to like him and trusted him for his building and carpentry skills and his integrity. Finkel, probably drawing on his childhood development of thrift in Ohio, let his savings grow.

The Growing Family

A little less than two years into the marriage, while the Italianate-style Columbia County Courthouse was under construction and the town of Dayton was on a building surge, Frank and Delia had their first son, Ben, born on November 9, 1887, a bright, healthy boy destined to eventually spend 12 years in the Idaho state legislature.

Elmer, a dark, slender, good-natured child, was born two years later. Clarence, born in 1893, died as an infant later that same year. But in 1900 Frank and Delia had a daughter and named her Theresia,

Lone Pine School District, Dayton, Washington
L-R, seated: 1?, 2?, Lloyd Rainwater, Robert Rainwater, Ben Finkel, Louella Hunt, Flora Mock (married Ben Finkel), Jessie Rainwater, 9? standing: 1?, Bernard Rainwater, Ralph Hunt, teacher, 5?, 6?, Leonard Rainwater, Arnold Mock

The Weinhard Saloon and Lodge Hall

odd spelling and all, after Frank's only sister from the old farm in Ohio.

Delia's marriage to the "German" Finkel worked out well. The extended Rainwater family, with Frank Finkel as a collateral member, became a regular force on the small-town economics of Dayton, a community commonly held by the turn of the century to be one of the prettiest towns in Washington state.[10]

Noteworthy Success

Frank kept a close eye on the bottom line. In 1903, he bought a farm for $950, worked the land for a year, probably made a good profit when the harvest came in, and then sold it for $1,000 in 1904[11] Since transactions were mostly in gold, and there was no income tax before 1913, the paper trail consists mostly of these land sales and deeds with clerk's signatures. By the first years of the 20th Century, Frank Finkel was a comparatively wealthy man by small-town standards.

Jacob Weinhard

Finkel's success was above the median, but far from unique. Jacob Weinhard, German-born and a citizen of Dayton, arrived from Portland, Oregon about the same time that Finkel arrived from the Little Big Horn by way of St. Louis. He had turned his brewery and barley fields into a burgeoning financial gold mine. By 1904, Weinhard owned the brewery, a malt house, the Weinhard Saloon and Lodge Hall, the Weinhard Theatre, and a piece of the Citizens National Bank of Dayton. He was a big man in town. In 1907, Weinhard built a mansion from the profits of the beer business and other transactions and investments. Jacob Rainwater, who had come to Oregon by ox-drawn wagon, was also a multiple property owner.

During this time of growth in Dayton, each June 25th of every fifth year following the Battle of the Little Big Horn, commemorative events marking the occasion were held across the nation recalling Custer's Last Stand, with staged battles pitting noble cavalrymen and savage Indians against each other, the former sacrificing their lives so the nation could live. Words of patriotism flowed from featured speakers and bands would play stirring music to capture the patriotic spirit of the throngs. Custer's defeat had taken on a fervor of almost religious magnitude. These dusty blood-and-gunpowder events with nostalgia flooding the souls of the attended on the anniversary date of the battle of the Little Big Horn had grown to mythical proportions across the nation.

Commemorations of the Little Big Horn now took place at regular intervals, but Frank Finkel stayed away from them.[12] The secret he harbored was obviously very present in his mind and his "lack of interest" in attending such anniversary events was possibly an indication that he was trying to avoid stirring up memories and quiet fears of being branded "a deserter in the face of the enemy."

The ability to hold a secret is fundamental to healthy social development, some psychologists maintain.[13] Frank Finkel's rise to success was a reflection of that ability. But time has a way of cooling the temperament and the mind cannot remain unchanged as it accumulates experiences. The ability to stay quiet in the face of misinformation, when the truth was known to him, appeared to undergo that change. Finkel was not, by nature, a modest man,[14] and perhaps it was his healthy ego that made it difficult to stay quiet when the misinformation about Custer's Last Stand was presented to him in some fashion.

When World War I occurred, and turned the world into a new place, it may, along with the distance in time, have softened Finkel's mindset about his deserter status and allowed it to rise to his conscious mind. The Army he had been in was the Army of history, lost in the mists of time. His impulsive reaction to correct misinformation about the Battle at the Little Big Horn provoked two impulsive responses. Frank was having some difficulty holding firm when the Indians were charged with a sneak attack or some other readily accepted falsehood. As a rule Frank stayed away from those events but he did attend one staged at Dayton's Dreamland Theater during the war. Typically, it was a misconstrued Custer's Last Stand. Upon leaving, he was overheard muttering by his companion, Robert Johnson, "That's not the way it was at all..." It wasn't until after Frank's admission and subsequent celebrity that Johnson realized that he was hearing the real story from an actual participant. [15]

His focus on a life of steady success through building, farming, shrewd investments, and thrift that he started when he arrived in Dayton by stagecoach ahead of the railroad was, if nothing else, a diversion from any fearful thoughts he may have had about the day he left his comrades of the 7th Cavalry in the valley of the Little Big Horn.

When he announced his retirement in 1905, his success did not go unnoticed, he made certain of it. He wrote or perhaps dictated a piece and submitted it to the *History of Southeastern Washington*, published the same year.

> "It is no small thing to enter a wild country and open a farm and it requires no mean judgment to be able to handle the property successfully and pass through the panics that have swept the country, maintaining a successful issue throughout it all. The subject of this article has done this and is to be classed with the leading and substantial men of the country. At present Mr. Finkel is residing in Dayton, Washington, and from his home place gives attention to the oversight of his property throughout the county. He has a fine estate of four hundred and eighty acres, choice farm land, which has been improved with everything needed.
>
> "The income from this property constitutes a handsome annual dividend. Mr. Finkel also gives attention to the handling of some live stock which brings him a revenue. He comes from staunch German ancestry, being the son of Peter and Lena (Windel) Finkel. He was born in Washington County, Ohio, on January 29, 1854. The parents were natives of Germany and came to this country when young. They settled in Ohio and there remained, substantial and well-to-do farmers, until their deaths. They raised a family of seven children named as follows: Henry, Peter, Frank, Charles, Adam, Joseph, and Theresia. The parents maintained a reputation

for uprightness and integrity which was a fine legacy
for their descendents.

"The first fifteen years of our subject's life were
in Washington County and there he gained his edu-
cational training from the country schools. At that
time he departed from the parental roof, journeying
to Wisconsin and Iowa, where he worked for four
or five years.

"He then took a trip by rail to the Golden
Gate. After looking over the prospects in California
he came on up through Oregon to the state of
Washington. He located here in Columbia County
in 1879. For a time he was occupied in smelter work
for Evans Gay. After that he took a trip to Spokane
and through the Big Bend country, after which he
was more convinced than ever that the proper place
to locate was near Dayton. Consequently he secured four hundred and eighty acres of land there.

Frank and Delia with their children
standing: Elmer, Ben; front row: Frank, Frank W., Delia, Theresia

Courtesy of Milton Koch

Frank W. and Theresia

From that time on until the day of his retirement he was known as one of the industrious and successful agriculturalists of the county. By economy and wisdom he laid by, or accumulated, a comfortable fortune."[16]

There is an obvious element of self-satisfaction in Finkel's saga that starts with the first sentence. He interestingly omits that period prior to his time in California and subsequent arrival in Dayton. If he had included his military service with the 7th Cavalry, he would also have to admit that he was technically a deserter. It is also interesting to note that he did not admit his parents had financial difficulties but indicates that they were well-to-do.

This self-generated piece indicates that Frank Finkel of Washington County, Ohio, is listed in the 1860 U.S. Census as the third son of Peter and Magdalena (Lena) (Windel) Finkle.

Note: The parental names and the birth order of the first five brothers in the account match perfectly. Joseph appears to have been born but not yet christened, and Theresia was not yet born in 1860.

After the Announcement

Although Finkel was retired, he kept on maintaining the house, overseeing the harvesting when family, in-laws, and friends would gather to bring in the crops, and working land swaps for solid profits, he also remained active as a husband, becoming the father of another child, Frank W. Finkel, sired when he was 50. Young Frank developed heart disease and died at age nine.

The year 1917, when the United States declared war on Germany and Austria-Hungary, was a dynamic year for Frank Finkel, as it was for wheat farmers throughout America. Wheat prices had rocketed from $1.44 a bushel to $3.25, sending the Chicago Board of Trade into shock; but unlike the Stock Exchange in New York, Chicago did not close its doors. A frantic Washington government quickly set up and opened the doors of the United States Grain Corporation.

Ben, Frank, Theresia, Delia, Elmer

Wheat prices opened at $2.44. With zones and agencies established as terminal points, Frank Finkel and the farmers of Washington were directed to bring their crop to the government agency at Portland, Oregon for shipment to the Great Lakes or the East Coast.

Profits were rolling in to the wheat farmers of America. Expansion was exponential, farm acreage grew, sales of farm equipment skyrocketed, tractor sales rising from 29,670 in 1916 to 203,207 in the four years through 1920. Companies like Chicago's International Harvester, owned by the heirs of J.P. Morgan, shared in the bonanza as its machines rolled out the factory doors and onto the farm fields of America. It is easy to envision a flood of farmers traveling to Chicago to see the newest mechanical marvels that were changing the American farming life; records indicate that Frank Finkel was one of them.

Chicago was a familiar town to Frank. He had enlisted there, lived there before his enlistment although it is not known how long, and before the Great War, Frank had occasions to visit Chicago and may have seen someone who knew his secret, an old adversary from the Little Big Horn, Rain-in-the Face, who appeared at the Chicago Exhibition in 1893.

Delia's Will

Frank and Delia Finkel had made a good marriage despite the fact that they married when he was 32 and she was 18. Perhaps being married to an older man, the death of her own mother, the death of Jake Rainwater in 1906, and the sad loss of young Frank, who died in 1912 when he was only nine, had given Delia an early maturity or some insights into the uncertainties of life. She took the precaution of making out a will, even though she and Frank owned everything jointly, when she was only 48 years old and in good health.

The World War was raging. The year was 1916—two years after the "Rape of Belgium" and one year after a U-Boat sank the *Lusitania* and the Germans notoriously and obtusely shot Edith Cavell [17] for espionage. This date may explain an odd fact about Delia's last will and testament: the typed document obviously spelled out the name

Be It Remembered, That, I, Delila Finkel, of the city of Dayton, County of Columbia and state of Washington, of the age of forty-eight years and being of sound and disposing mind and memory and not acting under duress, menace, fraud or undue influence of any person whomsoever, do make, publish and declare this my last will and testament in the manner following, that is to say:

First. I direct that my deceased body be decently buried with proper regard to my station in life and the circumstances of my estate and that my executor hereinafter named as soon as he shall have sufficient funds in his hands pay my funeral expenses and the expenses of my last sickness and my debts.

Second. I give and bequeath to my beloved children, Bennie Finkel, Elmer Finkel, sons and Theresia Finkel, daughter, the sum of one dollar each.

Third. I give, bequeath and devise all of the rest, residue and remainder of my estate, both real and personal of whatever name, kind or nature or where ever situate, together with the tenements, hereditaments, and appurtenances thereunto belonging or in anywise appertaining to my beloved husband Frank Finkel, forever.

Fourth. I hereby nominate and appoint my said husband Frank Finkel, the sole executor of this my last will and testament and direct that no bond shall be required of him as such and I hereby revoke all former wills by me made.

Fifth. I herein expressly provide that my estate shall be settled in the manner herein provided and that letters testamentary or of administration shall not be required to be issued and that after the probate of this my last will and testament and after the filing in the court of a true inventory of all of my estate and property, my estate shall be settled in the manner herein provided in all respects without further intervention of the courts.

In Witness Whereof, I have hereunto set my hand and seal this 21-day of March A.D. 1916.

Delila Finkel

Delia's Will

"Finkle" seven times, and each time someone had covered the last two letters and turned the name into "Finkel" with pen and ink.[18]

What's in a Name

Finkel had been using that spelling consistently since the turn of the century, but he never seemed to have objected when somebody shifted back to "Finkle," the most common spelling before 1900. Delia's husband and her stepmother were both German-American, but she herself was a Southerner, Anglo-Saxon and Scots-Irish—her mother's maiden name was Lucinda Williamson—with a touch of Cherokee. Jacob Rainwater, in fact, numbered a German who had emigrated to America in 1776 as the founder of the family. But names having to do with rain are frequent among Cherokee or mixed-Cherokee families. Delia's sisters were all married to men with names like Dale, Gibson, and Pettijohn. Was she trying to distance herself from the Beasts of Berlin? Or had the whole family gotten together and decided to fix the spelling of the name once and for all, purely for convenience sake?

By 1917—the year the United States went to war with Germany—Frank Finkel's name was, with some regularity, spelled as Finkel. Frank and Delia sold a big consolidated farm for $35,000 in 1917, with the provision that their son Ben Finkel retain the lease until November 1, 1918, when the harvest would be in and the crops sold at high wartime prices.[19]

By 1920, the census showed that Frank and Delia had three living children: Ben was 33 and lived in Idaho with his wife Flora, Elmer was 30 and lived in Dayton, and Theresia, their daughter, was 20, still at home, and soon to be married into the Koch family of Dayton.[20]

Ben, who had inherited some of his father's restless spirit, was farming in Idaho, trying to do what his father had done in Washington State. Frank Finkel's older brothers Henry and Peter, meanwhile, had come to live in Dayton, where the Finkels and the Rainwaters were a local dynasty of some influence and respect, and had moved in next door.

Ben Finkel

Frank and Delia Finkel, with 480 acres of good farmland and $40,000 in gold-backed greenbacks[21] were moderately wealthy and well-respected citizens of Dayton, backed by some of the most prominent and prosperous in-laws in town and the account of his life in the *History Of Southeastern Washington Journal* would have appeared to make Frank Finkel's life an "open book to the casual reader." But it was not. He was a man of secrets.

Notes
[1]Dyer, Robert L., "A Brief History Of Steamboating On The Missouri River," *Boonslick Historical Society Quarterly,* June, 1997.
[2]*Bismarck Tribune,* issue of July 6, 1876, full front-page account of "Custer Massacre" with a list of known casualties.
[3]Finkel File, Oshkosh Public Museum, various accounts by Finkel's second wife in mostly undated newspaper clippings. Hermie, the second wife, committed herself to fabrications that Frank had joined the Army under an assumed name and otherwise confused the legal aspects of his military service beyond recognition. Jealousy of the late Delia may have been a motivating factor.
[4]Dyer, Robert L., *A Brief History Of Steamboating.*

[5]Finkel File, Oshkosh Public Museum.

[6]"A History Of Dayton," a pamphlet from the Dayton Chamber of Commerce describing the history of Dayton, also the source of all subsequent facts about the history of the town.

[7]Columbia County Courthouse, public records. The marriage book, which contains the spelling of the original name "Finckle," could not be placed on the copying machine.

[8]Finkel File, Oshkosh Public Museum. Alternatively, Hermie Sperry Finkel, Finkel's second wife, appears to have minimized Delia's knowledge of his military service. Most likely, Finkel told Delia everything but pledged her to silence, which she kept as long as he did.

[9]Columbia County Courthouse, public records, and conversations with Faye Rainwater, Jacob Rainwater's granddaughter-in-law. "They weren't what you would call rich, but he was a good farmer—they did all right."

[10]Columbia County Courthouse, public records.

[11]*Ibid.*

[12]Finkel File, Oshkosh Public Museum, newspaper clipping of March 20, 1921. Frank said he wouldn't be going to the commemoration that summer in Montana, even after he'd gone public with his role as a survivor and was believed implicitly by most of his neighbors.

[13]New York Times, January 11, 2005

[14]See page 72

[15]Finkel File, Oshkosh Public Museum.

[16]Finkel File, Oshkosh Public Museum. The history Frank Finkel was interviewed for was never actually published but a copy was provided by Dr. Arthur Kannenberg, who placed it in the Finkel File at the Oshkosh Public Museum.

[17] *The Grolier Libary Of World War I,* Volume 3, pages 110-113. Edith Cavell, 49, a British nurse and nursing instructor working n Brussels, Belgium, at the outbreak of the war, was arrested and tried for helping about 200 British, French and Belgian prisoners-of-war of the Germans to escape back to the Allied lines. She pleaded guilty to the charge and was shot by a German firing squad on October 12, 1915. Cavell's treatment had been strict but correct and the Kaiser himself had opposed her execution, which was legal under military law but widely resented because she was a woman of excellent character, deeply religious, and not involved in violent sabotage. The execution caused outrage in Allied countries, in Spain, and in the United States, and helped tip American sentiment, once largely neutral, to become more anti-German.

[18]Columbia County Courthouse, Last Will and Testament of Delila Finkel. Delia or Delila used both names alternatively. Her husband's name and the land plots confirm she was the same person. Delia me-

thodically corrected the last two typed letters in the name "Finkle" to
"Finkel" with pen and ink seven separate times on two pages.

[19]Columbia County Courthouse, public records.

[20]U.S. Census of 1920.

[21]Prior to 1935 all U.S. paper money could be redeemed for gold or silver,
but many people, farmers and Westerners in particular, preferred to deal
in gold coins for large transactions and silver for daily expenses.

Chapter Seven

The Admission

The clink of horseshoes against the iron stake at the Finkel farm and the cluck of chickens scratching for food must have sounded soothing and peaceful in early April of 1920. The Great War had been over for 17 months, life before it seemed to be a different world away.

Winter was gone and the infusion of spring rains was bringing the landscape back to life. It was a gathering of the friends of Delia and Frank Finkel, most in their Sunday best after attending Sunday services. Jake Rainwater, who had lived next door before he died some years before, had customarily stopped in on Sunday, the "day off." Everyone relaxed unless some kind of bind intruded so it was a good time to get together.

The grown-up men removed their suit coats and vests and played horseshoes in shirtsleeves while the children played the usual childhood games and Delia, her sisters, and the other women sat around the front yard talking or laying out food on the table. It was the kind of day that even horses in harness would enjoy one another's company under the shade of the trees, chomping and swishing their tails.

This was the first year of Prohibition and the law only prevented selling alcohol, not drinking it, and the nearby brewery may have made that stipulation when providing the group with its brew. Whatever, the beer was at hand and appreciated on that April day when the church-going men were attired in Sunday-best woolen suits and boiled shirts.

Then, as voices arose amid the clinking horseshoes, Frank Finkel's ears picked out some words from a nearby voice that did something to him. They hit a nerve.

Somebody started talking about what the "damn Indians" did to General Custer.

Frank reacted, thinking of Delia's Cherokee heritage, and turned toward the voice and admonished the man who had uttered them. He didn't like talk about "damn Indians" in front of Delia.

"What the hell do you know about General Custer?" Frank blurted.[1]

"I know as much about it as you do," the neighbor said.

"The hell you do...," Frank snorted.

"How do you know so much about it, Frank?" his neighbor asked.

"I was there!" Frank said bluntly. It was out. The secret he hid for 44 years was no longer a secret. It was now wide open. He must have felt a relief.

"What do you mean you were there? Where?"

"Custer's Last Stand!" Frank said, perhaps not believing he finally opened up on the subject. No good backing down now.

"The hell you were! Everybody got killed that day!"

"I didn't!" Frank said, veins in his neck probably bulging as he beckoned the small crowd to him. He bent over and pulled up his trouser leg.

"Here, look at this!"

There it was! The gunshot wound, pink after 40-odd years but still a blister just to the left of the shin bone.

"That's a gunshot wound all right!" one of the neighbors said.

"Come back to the house!" Frank commanded.

The men, falling in line, marched back to the front door, striding past the bewildered women who stared at them beneath wrinkled brows.

Frank stopped the trooping men at the door. They became a small crowd bunching up as Frank hurriedly rushed to the rear bedroom. He pulled open a drawer on a dark oaken chest and excitedly groped around, pushing aside fabric—sweaters, shirts, underwear—then he felt the smooth texture of old paper.

He walked outside to the small crowd of men in boiled white shirts and wide ties. They closed in around him and watched with curiosity as Finkel slowly, carefully, unfolded a packet of papers. Then he held up a creased copy of the *Bismarck Tribune* and two letters somebody had sent him addressed to:

Frank Finkel,

7th Cavalry,

Fort Abraham Lincoln, Dakota Territory.[2]

As Finkel handed the letters and the old newspaper around he had to feel a swirl of emotion. Perhaps relief at the revelation itself, but the satisfaction of telling the story as it actually happened had to be foremost in his mind. It was the inaccuracy of his neighbor's story that had prompted him to blurt out that he *was* at the battle.

But it had to feel good to get it out.

His neighbors all thought the Little Big Horn fight was some kind of "Sioux ambush." Finkel knew the reality. It was planned to be a 7th Cavalry surprise attack. He remembered the surprise on himself, *the troopers, dog-weary after the night march, walking their horses in the dark, stumbling over rocks and rattling stones in their tin cups so they didn't wander off into Indian country,* and then the attack. It happened so quickly. It must have seemed like a blur. The excited comments by his neighbors possibly intermingled with traces of awe may have triggered his memory bank to open as the neighbors read and re-read the letters and the creased copy on the front page of the *Bismarck Tribune* with hungry eyes.

Perhaps it was faces, long gone, that poured up from the recesses of his mind. Names like Bobo, Finley, Windolph, Kanipe. Short, Martini. Then perhaps he heard screams… he must have remembered the panic in the Indian village as he told the real story to his neighbors: the women running around screaming and dragging their children and how the warriors first showed up once the firing started.

Ambush!

He knew the Sioux were sleeping. He knew what happened. Yes, he knew. He was there. He was there.

Notes

[1] Finkel File, Oshkosh Public Museum. Frank's second wife, Hermie, told the same story—consistently—to reporters from three different newspapers and later, to various government officials she contacted by mail.

[2] *Ibid.* The story in the *Walla Walla Union Bulletin* of March 20, 1921 says: "Frank Finkel, of this town, declares he was there and his story is borne out by the name 'Finkle' on the regiment's roster, and by various residents of Dayton who say they have seen papers, since lost in a fire, which proved the fact."

Chapter Eight

Life in Public View

A few days after his admission to being a survivor of the battle at the Little Big Horn, Frank Finkel was constructing a new porch on the front of his house. While he was attempting to cut though some planks he had laid out on two sawbucks in the front yard, two neighbors who had been at the horseshoe match when Finkel admitted to being at the Little Big Horn approached him. A husky young blonde Swedish man in blue overalls was with them.

"Frank, we want you to come to the Kiwanis meeting and tell what you told us on Sunday—it's mighty interesting."

"I can't make it," Frank said. "I'm busy with this porch."

"Come on, Frank, you're the biggest man in Dayton."

"You're thinking of my father-in-law, God rest his soul," Frank said. "I'm not even the tallest man in Dayton—not hardly."

"Frank, I got a bet riding on this," one of his friends said. "We want you to tell them what you told us."

"I can't make it—I got to fix the porch."

"We all chipped in to hire a carpenter to do it for you," one neighbor said. The young Swede in overalls grinned and flexed the muscle in his right arm.

"The hell…" Frank said.

He was shy about public speaking, wondered how Ben had ever gotten interested in politics. But still…

"Can I bring Delia?" he asked. Delia liked to eat in a restaurant now and then. Frank didn't much care for it. Delia was a good cook.

"Kiwanis is only for men," one of the neighbors said.

Frank nodded reflectively. "OK."

It wasn't a secret anymore. It was out. It was a story about a different world, about an Army that didn't exist anymore. No harm now.

And Frank was not a modest man. The attention was not unwelcome.

The lunch took place at Weinhard's Restaurant, with heavy German carved furniture, heavy German food, and enough beer to overcome Frank's dislike of public speaking.

Paintings of the Old Pacific Northwest dominated the walls.[1] Frank wished Delia could have come, she would have enjoyed the occasion and he would have liked to see her familiar face.

John "Doc" Summers was there, and Frank liked seeing him. Summers was in Congress and had been in the State Legislature for three years.

After the luncheon, Frank stood up to speak. The members of the crowd, Dayton's solid citizens, listened attentively. They knew they were hearing something special and they embraced Frank and his story. He was Frank Finkel, who never lied. He was Dayton's own.

The article following the Kiwanis luncheon appeared in the April 8 issue of the local newspaper:

> Dayton, April 8.—Frank Finkel, a pioneer resident of Columbia county, was the chief speaker at the Thursday luncheon of the Dayton Kiwanis Club this week. He was eye witness to the Custer Massacre and gave to the club the account of his thrilling escape and the circumstances which pre-

vented the knowledge of his survival from reaching the government at the time. Congressman John W. Summers of Walla Walla was a guest at the luncheon and he will make an effort to get government recognition of Mr. Finkel's story.

In giving the account of the battle in which General Custer's command was pocketed by the Indian forces Mr. Finkel said his horse became "kettler" and bolted through the Indian lines, carrying him to a territory beyond the fighting. He had two serious bullet wounds and after many days of wandering he found a cabin in the wilderness where he was months recovering from his injuries."[2]

Nobody who knew Frank Finkel doubted he'd been there—the journalist obviously didn't understand when Finkel used the term "*skedaddled*" and wrote "*kettler*," but the Civil War slang term for a panicked flight brands Finkel as a veteran of the Old Army. Down home in Dayton, Frank was the goods.

The story traveled, at least around southern Washington, and Frank Finkel became a hard-working home-town celebrity.

On June 25, 1921, the 45th anniversary of the Battle of the Little Big Horn was marked with ceremonies in Montana. Elizabeth Custer didn't go to the ceremonies at the battlefield.

"I have never been back to Montana since that day," Custer's widow told the newspapers in 1921 in New York City, where she lived on Park Avenue. "I just couldn't go," she said, adding to the mythology of national sacrifice, "but I am with this western spirit. Progress and development were the things for which General Custer gave his life. And that is the spirit of the west today."

Frank Finkel didn't go either. But the newspapers in Washington State spoke to Frank Finkel again and took photographs of him standing on the new porch, just a little bow-legged and favoring one side a little as he posed for the camera while chomping a big cigar.

"*The battle opened with an attack on an Indian village*," Finkel told the reporter. "*General Custer led one set of troops while Major (Marcus) Reno headed another.*[3]

Newspaper accounts of Frank's story.

CUSTER MEMORIAL TO BE ERECTED
WASHINGTON MAN CLAIMS TO B E ONLY MASSACRE SURVIVOR *1921*

(By Newspaper Enterprise.)

Dayton, Wash., June 25.—Of the five companies of soldiers who fought with General George A. Custer at the famous massacre on the Little Big Horn on June 25, 1876, not one man survived. That is what history says.

But Frank Finkle, of this town, declares he was there and his story is borne out by the name "Finkle" on the regiment's roster, and by various residents of Dayton who say they have seen papers, lost since in a fire, which proved the fact.

All this is why Finkle is being urged to attend ceremonies to be held at Hardin, Mont., on June 25, the forty-fifth anniversary of the massacre.

Finkle, a member of the troops commanded by Capt. Tom Custer, brother of the famous general, relates how the regiment took up the trail of Sitting Bull and his warriors.

"The battle opened with an attack on an Indian village," he says. "General Custer led one set of troops while Major Reno headed another.

"Custer's forces rode on to the attack until suddenly there was a thunder of yells as the Sioux Indians sprang from behind every bush and poured over the hilltops.

"Men and horses fell all around me. A bullet hit my rifle stock and a splinter of steel started blood flowing between my eyes. My horse bolted and carried me, half blinded, through the Indian lines.

"Then came a stinging sensation in my shoulder, and I lost consciousness, falling forward on my horse. When I came to, it was dark. Early next morning I reached the mountains.

"For five days I rode, eating raw rabbits in fear of attracting the Indians if I built a fire.

"On the sixth day I met some trappers, and stayed with them until September. Then I rode back to Fort Benton and was discharged."

Memorial Erected.

Harding, Mont., June 25.—A monument to Gen. George A. Custer and his soldiers will be unveiled here on June 25, during the 45th anniversary observance of the Custer Massacre. The famous battle will be re-enacted and Indians who took part in the original fight will direct the production, some of them taking actual part.

Extra on Massacre.

Bismark, N. D., June 25.—The first printed account of the Custer Massacre of 1876, was an "extra" issued by the Bismark Tribune. It was a one sheet affair and sold for 25 cents. It didn't appear until July 6, eleven days after the battle.

Mrs. Custer Author.

New York, June 25.—Mrs. Elizabeth Bacon Custer, widow of General Custer, has been urged to attend the 45th anniversary observance of the Custer Massacre, at Hardin, Mont., June 25. But she will not go.

"I have never been back to Montana since that day," she says. "I just couldn't go. But I am with this western spirit. Progress and development were the things for which General Custer gave his life. And that is the spirit of the west today."

Mrs. Custer has written three books dealing with her western ...

General Custer, battle scene, and full length picture of Frank Finkle, who says he's sole survivor of massacre.

Newspaper accounts of Frank's story.

Delia's Death Certificate

Custer's forces rode on to the attack, until suddenly there was a thunder of yells as the Sioux Indians sprang from behind every bush and poured over the hilltops.

Men and horses went down all around me. A bullet hit my rifle stock and a splinter of steel started blood flowing between my eyes. My horse bolted and carried me, half-blinded, through the Indian lines.

Then came a stinging sensation in my shoulder, and I lost consciousness, falling forward on my horse. When I came to, it was dark. Early next morning I reached the mountains.

For five days I rode, eating raw rabbits in fear of attracting the Indians if I built a fire.

On the sixth day I met some trappers and stayed with them until September...."

Finkel did not hesitate about being the Finkle on the 7th Cavalry casualty list, and the Finckle on the 1872 enlistment form.

"Of the five companies of soldiers who fought with General George A. Custer at the famous massacre on the Little Big Horn on June 25, 1876, not one man survived," a newspaper reporter wrote in Dayton. *"That is what history says. But Frank Finkel, of this town, declares he was there, and his story is borne out by the regiment's roster and by various residents of Dayton who say they have seen papers, lost since in a fire, which proved this fact."*

Delia's Death

The biggest chapter in Frank's old world suddenly opened up while the biggest chapter in his new life was coming to an end. Delia took ill and died.

Delia may have sensed when she filled out her detailed will in 1916 that she would go before Frank did, even though she married Frank when she was still a teenager and he was a work-hardened man of 32. Without much advanced warning, Delia Finkel died in August of 1921, after a brief illness, of acute endocarditis.

"Her husband, who survived her, was the only soldier who escaped the Custer massacre," the obituary blandly noted[4].

She was survived by Frank and their three living children, Theresia, Elmer, and Ben Finkel, her brother, Preston Rainwater of

In the Superior Court of the State of Washington for the County of
Columbia.

    In the Matter of the Estate of :   Affidavit as to Heirs and Devisees

    Delila Finkel, Deceased.   :   And no Other or Subsequent Will.

                                :

No R31

FILED

OCT 2 3 1921

at 11 25 o'clock A. M.

State of Washington,

County of Columbia. SS.

    Frnak Finkel, being first duly sworn on oath says:

That he has heretofore and on this day, made and filed in the above entitled court his petition duly verified, praying therein for the probate
of a certain written instrument purporting to be the last will and testament of the said deceased, Delila Finkel, as and for the last will of the
the said deceased and the appointment of himself as the sole executor
thereof; That to the bset of his knowledge and belief there is no other
or subsequent will of deceased, and that the said instrument so purporting
is the last will and testament of said deceased; and that the ages , relationship to the said deceased, and post office address of the heirs and
devisees of said deceased are as follows:

Frank Finkel, age 67 years, residence and post office address Dayton
Washington, and surviving husband of deceased; Rennie Finkel, age 24
residence and post office address Mohler, Idaho, and surviving son of said
deceased; Elmer Finkel, age 31 ,residence and post office address Dayton
Washington, and surviving son of said deceased; Theresia Finkel, age 22
residence and post office address, Dayton Washington, and surviving daughter of said deceased;

    That this affiant knows of no other or subsequent will of deceased.

                             Frank Finkel

Delia's Probate Certificate

13 Aug. 1921

Mrs. Frank Finkle

Mrs. De Lila Almightala whter Finkle wife of Mr. Frank Finkle of this city, died Tuesday at 10:30 p. m. at the family home after only a few days illness. She was daughter of Jacob Rainwater and was born in Oregon February 23 1868. The family settled on Robinett mountain, a few miles from this city, many years ago, and the deceased had lived in this city and county ever since. Her husband, who survives her, was the only soldier who escaped the Custer massacre. Besides her husband she is survived by a daughter, Theresa Finkle and two sons, Ben Finkle of Nez Perce, Idaho, and Elmer Finkle of this city. She is also survived by a brother, Preston Rainwater, of this county, and three sisters, Mrs. Al Dale and Mrs. Joseph Gibson of this city and Mrs. Dyer Pettyjohn of Twin Falls, Idaho.

The funeral will be held Thursday at 2:30 from the Christian church in this city.

#1213 Obituary of Delilah Rainwater Finkle,
13 Aug 1921, Columbia Co., Washington newspaper,
photocopy, from Ray Rainwater

Delia's Obituary

Dayton, and her three married sisters, Mrs. Al Dale and Mrs. Joseph Gilmore of Dayton, and Mrs. Dyer Pettijohn of Twin Falls, Idaho. The funeral took place at the Christian Church of Dayton, where her step-mother Nellie, Jacob Rainwater's second wife and mother of nine children, was active in the church and in the Women's Relief Corps.

Signing off on the wife who had come to him as a teenaged bride when he was a stranger looking over his shoulder, and had helped him build a strong family and a small fortune in land and gold, Finkel's hand shook when he wrote his name at the bottom of the probate certificate. But the slant of the penmanship, the Germanic construction of the capital F, the cluttered top of the letter K, and the tight loops on the E and the L indicate that, despite a gap of 49 years of mostly manual labor, the hand that signed the 1921 probate certificate in Dayton was the same hand that signed the 1872 enlist-ment form in Chicago.

The probate of Delia's will—by now, the clerk was erroneously spelling her name Delilah—was simple and direct, thanks to the will she had made out four years before, with the seven changes in the name spelling from "Finkle" to "Finkel." Each of the three surviving children received a token bequest of $1, and Delia left the remainder of her estate *"to my beloved husband, Frank Fink(el), forever."*[5]

Notes
[1]Shellie McLeod of Weinhard's, in Dayton, provided the author with some vintage photographs and a menu from the 1920s.
[2]Finkel File, Oshkosh Public Museum, newspaper story from April 8, 1920, clipped so that the newspaper cannot be definitely identified.
[3]Finkel File, Oshkosh Public Museum, *Walla Walla Union Bulletin*, Washington, March 20, 1921.
[4]Finkel File, Oskosh Public Museum, obituary of Delia Rainwater Finkel, from a Columbia County newspaper, donated by Rainwater family.
[5]Columbia County Courthouse, Probate of Delia Finkel's Last Will and Testament.

Chapter Nine

The Final Years

Life without Delia gave Frank a sense of loss but also a sense of freedom, not one he may have welcomed, but one that he hadn't experienced in decades. Frank was financially comfortable and had a huge extended family in Dayton, including his brothers Henry and Peter and Delia's brother and sisters and her nine half-brothers and half-sisters. He administered the farms, and the family ran things. Being a shrewd man, he had to keep abreast of new developments in farm equipment, which in the 1920s were improving quickly. He must have found it necessary to go to the centers of development. Chicago was prominent in that industry and he knew Chicago well. He had been there more than once or twice.

After five years elapsed following Delia's death, a train from Chicago pulled into the Dayton depot and a lady alighted onto the platform. Her name was Herminie C. Sperry, a resident of Chicago. She was in Dayton to reacquaint with a friend. The friend was Frank Finkel.

Born in Canada in January, 1864, Herminie Sperry was a corporate career woman who hit the glass ceiling, which was firmly in

The depot in Dayton, Washington.

place directly over the ground floor at that time. She had worked for Armour and Company, the meat packers, for 25 years. She began as a stenographer in May 1901 in Hartford, Connecticut, transferred to Cincinnati, Ohio and then to the meat packer's main office in Chicago. She retired after 25 years, in May, 1926 and apparently bought a train ticket to Dayton upon leaving the office. Less than a month later, she and Frank Finkel were married.[1]

A woman living in the Edwardian era, not in the state of matrimony nor with private and independent means, had to make her way with a strength of resolve in order to survive. That strength certainly had to develop within any woman with a desire to function in the corporate environment. Since direct power was not available to women in the corporate world, the development of unofficial power was necessary, and was a reflection of the woman's ability to get what she wanted.[2] A survival of 25 years in the corporate world in the Edwardian era and the turbulent years of World War I indicates that a woman such as Herminie Sperry had developed such inner strength, or initially had the resolve and knew how to get what she wanted, such as her eventual relocation to the corporate home office.

Frank and Herminie probably met on occasions in Chicago, but there is no record as to whether their relationship started before, or of how intense it may have been. Frank did visit the city frequently and was seen there by someone other than his business acquaintances and Hermie. An old adversary also saw him—Rain-in-the Face, the formidable Sioux chief, apparently saw Frank at the Chicago Exposition in 1893. Rain was part of an exposition featuring the actual cabin in which Sitting Bull was living when he was shot by Indian Police in 1890 during the outbreak of the tragic Ghost Dance. Several other Indians were in the exhibit but Rain-in-the-Face, the last great fighting chief from the Little Big Horn, was a star attraction. Frank, who

D.F. Barry and Rain-in-the-Face

obviously had difficulties admitting his Custer survivor "deserter" status, couldn't stay away, but he was noticed by someone who saw him on the battlefield, probably a woman from the Hunkpapa camp, who told Rain-in-the-Face.

The following year when he was at New York's Coney Island, Rain-in-the Face was interviewed by writer W. Kent Thomas, who asked about Curley, an Army Crow scout:

"Ugh! I know Curley. He is a liar," Rain told Thomas. "He never was in the fight. His horse stumbled and broke something. He stayed behind to fix it. When he heard the firing, he ran off like a whipped dog. One Long Sword escaped though; his pony ran off with him and went past our lodges. They told me about it at Chicago. I saw the man there, and I remember hearing the squaws telling about it after the fight."[3]

It is a matter of record, also, that Frank was in Chicago in 1914 on his way to visit his brothers and sister in Ohio. His daughter Theresia received a postcard from him. Frank signed the card with a soft lead pencil.

On June 28, 1926 Frank Finkel, the man Rain-in the-Face saw in Chicago a second time and Hermie, who obviously saw Frank

Frank and his surviving brothers and sister in 1914.

Postcard from Frank

in Chicago more often than twice, were married. She was 62 years old and Frank Finkel was 72.[4] They lived in Dayton and Herminic settled in rearranging furniture, curtains, replacing Delia's pictures, making the home her home, and as it appears, went about the business of changing the man as well.

Previously, Finkel had kept his investments relatively simple and close to home, farm land around Dayton and a sizable bank account. Most of his land sales were paid for in gold coins passed from hand to hand. In all, he bought or sold 10 farms, including one homestead where the land was free and bound to the owner by virtue of the improvements he made.

That changed when Hermie moved in. It was the 1920s and the investment world seemed to be a vast money churn. The Finkel portfolio expanded into mining stock and property in Montana. His wardrobe changed too. Once Finkel could be seen sporting a thick soldier's moustache and a trim soldier's beard, and was given to coarse-looking three-piece suits cut in the manner people sometimes called *Dutchy*—plain German with no pretensions to elegance— topped off with a dark fedora hat set at an angle, perhaps subliminally

Frank, c. 1921

recapturing a touch of the non-issue hats Captain Tom Custer had bought for the 7th Cavalry's C Company in St. Paul. The 7th Cavalry could never have been far from his mind, before or after that Sunday afternoon playing horseshoes.

When Delia was still alive, photographs show Frank Finkel with a soldier's stance, the cavalryman's bowed legs and chomping a cigar.[5] With Hermie in residence, Frank's wardrobe changed to better-tailored clothes; the "*Dutchy*" clothes disappeared, as did his facial hair—first the white beard, finally the "foreign-looking" flowing moustache.[6] There is no record that the cigars disappeared. What did appear was a housemaid. Hermie had taken over Frank's life. She was in possession. Only his children did not make him solely hers, but they were leaving the nest.

Two years after his second marriage, in 1928, at age 74, the man who rode a sorrel horse away from the Little Big Horn in 1876 splurged on a new Chevrolet Coupe for $500. He paid cash.

Hermie and Frank, c.1929

That same year, *National Geographic*, experimenting with color photography, ran a picture of some Lakota Indian men and women in tribal finery with the caption: "*No other tribe resisted the oncoming tide of the white man's civilization with more determination than the brave and aggressive Sioux. A well-equipped people, both physically and mentally, they were for many years monarchs of the country that is now Minnesota, the Dakotas and Montana. The ancestors of some of the chiefs pictured here planned and executed the campaign in which Custer's immortal band perished.*"[7]

If Frank had read that article in *National Geographic* he probably snorted and shook his head, and perhaps he smiled at the reference to "planned and executed."

In autumn the following year, 1929, the New York Stock Market crashed and wiped out some of Frank and Hermie's investments. The subsequent pain he felt was not just due to the financial loss. It was far more serious and it ran deep for months, the intensity rivaling the pain suffered by the wounded Second Sergeant that he once was. The doctor's diagnosis was stomach cancer.[8]

His decline was painful and after a bitter struggle of eight months, the man who had defeated pain and enflamed wounds in a Montana shack 54 years before lost the battle. With a yellow Chevrolet Coupe in his homestead, the man who rode horses to meet history in Montana and Wyoming died on August 28, 1930.

Hermie and Frank

Frank Finkel's signature on his last will and testament, three days before his death, shows a failing, shaky hand, the same hand that signed the enlistment form in 1872 and Delia's probate in 1921. [9] The distinctive capital F and the off-center dot on the letter I remained consistent even as his hand trembled. Frank managed to drag out the struggle to die in the same month that Delia had died nine years before. When he passed away he was 76 years of age. The lone survivor of the five Custer companies at the Little Big Horn had rejoined his comrades.

Settling the Estate

Frank Finkel's last will and testament showed how things had changed between Delia's death in 1921 and his own departure in 1930. Delia left the sons and daughter a dollar each and everything

Case no P 394

Be It Remembered, That I, Frank Finkel, of the city of Dayton County Of Columbia, State of Washington, of the age of seventy-six years and being of sound and disposing mind and memory, and not acting under duress, menace, fraud or undue influence, of any person whomsoever, do make, publish and declare this my last will and testament in manner following, that is to say:

First. I direct that my deceased body be decently buried with proper regard to my station in life and the circumstances of my estate, and that my executrix hereinafter named as soon as she shall have sufficient funds in her hands, pay my funeral expenses and the expenses of my last sickness and my debts.

Second. I give and bequeath to my children, Bennie Finkel, Elmer Finkel, sons, and Theresia Koch, daughter, the sum of one dollar each.

Third. I give, bequeath and devise all of the rest, residue and remainder of my estate, both real and personal of whatever, name, kind or nature or where ever situate, together with the tenements, hereditaments and appurtenances thereunto belonging or in anywise appertaining to my beloved wife, Hermie C. Finkel. Forever——————

Fourth. I hereby nominate and appoint my said wife, Hermie C. Finkel, the sole executrix of this my last will and testament and provide that no bond shall be required of her as such and I hereby revoke all former wills by me made.

Fifth. I herein expressly provide that my estate shall be settled in the manner herein provided and that letters testamentary or of administration shall not be required to be issued and that after the probate of this my last will and testament and after the filing in the court of a true inventory of all of my estate, and property, my estate be settled in all respects as herein provided without further intervention of the courts, except to make such orders as are required to be made in cases of non-intervention wills.

In Witness Whereof, I have hereunto set my hand and seal this 25th day of August A.D. 1930.

Frank Finkel

Frank's Will

else to her husband. Frank left Hermie the house and half of his bank account and gave one-sixth of the cash to each of his three children.

The Wall Street Crash had depleted Frank's cash position. At Delia's departure he had about $40,000 in gold alone, purchasing power of more than $1,000,000 in 21st Century money, along with the house and about a square mile of Dayton farmland. The fall of farm prices had made the wheat land in Montana a questionable investment, and the mining stock was worthless by the time Frank died. The property holdings had become a grim matter:

3,500 shares in the Chloride Queen Mine, bought at 30 cents a share, cash value zero; 3,500 shares in the Chloride Queen Mine, bought at 2 cents a share, cash value zero;

1 share in the Nisling Mining and Development Company, cash value zero.

Frank had also helped his son Ben get a start in life with a $4,000 loan in 1926; Ben signed a promissory note and agreed to pay back $200 a year in interest a few months after Frank married Hermie.

The payments on the promissory note were split four ways— half to Hermie and a sixth each to Ben, Elmer, and Theresia.

The Chevrolet Coupe was now valued at $350, and the house at $1,800, with $150 for household goods and furniture.

Additional land in Montana was valued at $5,000 and this went directly to Hermie. A time deposit in Columbia National Bank at 4 per cent interest came to $1,250, this also went to Hermie. The cash on hand was $568.25, plus Frank's gold watch and chain, valued at $7.50.

Not surprisingly, the relationship between Hermie and the Finkel sons and daughter became strained. The Chevrolet Coupe may have been the catalyst for hostility. Elmer, Finkel's second son, wanted his father's car but didn't have the cash on hand to buy it, or even pay for half of it. The three siblings worked out a deal among themselves and then approached Hermie.

Ben Finkel, Elmer Finkel and Theresia Finkel Koch each agreed to contribute one-sixth of the value of the car so Elmer could own it, which gave each of them only $64.89 in leftover cash from Frank's

In the Superior Court of the State of Washington for the County of
Columbia.   *P 394*   FILED

AT_____

In the Matter of the Estate of   ;
                                      ; Agreement.   JAN 31 1931
Frank Finkel Deceased.   ;
                                      ;;   J. F. CLANCY,
                                                                           COUNTY CLE
                                                                           By *Cora Morga* Dep

To the Honorable E. V. Kuykendall, ~Judge~ of the above entitled court;
Whereas the said Hermie C. Finkel, executrix of the will of Frank Finkel
deceased, and Bennie Finkel, Elmer Finkel and Theresia Koch, are the
owners jointly of the one Chevrolette Coupe model 1928 automobile in part
as follows; that said Hermie C. Finkel one-half, and the other threeowner
one-sixth each. and the said automobile is apartof the property of the
above named estate; and Whereas, the said owners and heirs are each desir
ous of sell *any* ~to~ the said ~automobile~ automobile to the said Elmer Finkel
for the sum of $ *350.00* ----- and he the said Elmer finkel as not sufficier
funds on hand to pay the said Hermie C. Finkel the sum of $ *175.00* ----which
is her amount of the purchase price. And whereas said estate will be
settled some time in the month of April 1931, or thereabouts, and at the
time of such settlement it is hereby agreed that the said Hermie C. Finke
is to be permited to deduct the sum of $ *175.00* ----from the total balance
of cash subject to distribution ~before any share or~ out of any money
coming to said Bennie Finkel, and Elmer Finkel and the said Theresia
Koch.

Dated January 31st 1931,

Bennie Finkel
~*Elmer Finkel*~
Mrs Theresia Koch
Hermie C. Finkel

The agreement regarding the Chevrolet Coupe

estate, while their stepmother got $354.68 cash in hand, the house, the farm, and the wheat land in Montana.[10]

Elmer also had to pay Hermie $10.00 for his father's box of carpenter tools.

Except for $204.67, Herminie had virtually taken possession of Frank's life after death.

Notes

[1]Finkel file, Oshkosh Public Museum.

[2]Heaphey, James, *How to Survive in an Organization.*

[3]Brady, Cyrus Townsend, *Indian Fights and Fighters*, page 291. Curley told essentially the same story through Russell White Bear just before he died in 1923, and Suzy Yellowtail, one of Curley's relatives and the first Crow woman to become an RN, confirmed it to the author and his wife in the 1970s. "He never went down in that valley at all. He wasn't that stupid." Rain spoke straight.

[4]Columbia County Courthouse, marriage certificate of Frank Finkel and Herminie Sperry Finkel.

[5]Finkel File, Oshkosh Public Museum. Photo taken in 1921 by *Walla Walla Union Bulletin*, as alternative to the photograph used in the article of March 20, 1921.

[6]*Ibid.* Photo of Herminie and Frank Finkle, no date, probably close to 1930.

[7]*National Geographic,* June issue of 1928, Plate XXIV opposite page 719, article "Photographic Marvels of the West In Color," photos by Fred Payne Clatsworthy.

[8]Columbia County Courthouse, Death Certificate of Frank Finkel.

[9]*Ibid*, Last Will and Testament of Frank Finkel, 1930.

[10]*Ibid*, probate of Last Will and Testment of Frank Finkel, 1930.

Frank's Death Certificate

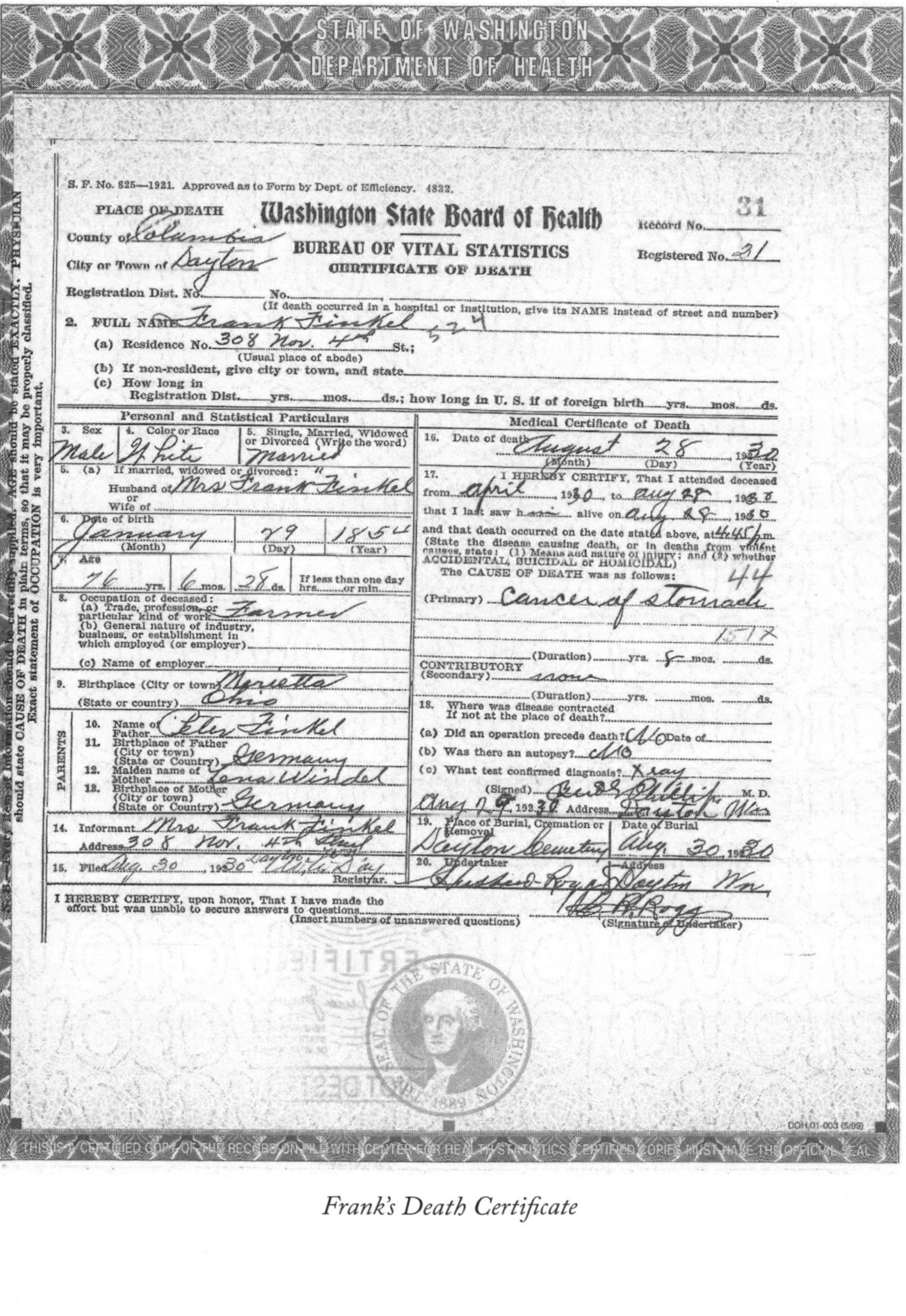

Part Two

The Experts, Pro and Con

Chapter Ten

Starting the Fire, Wrong Smoke Signals

When Frank Finkel was buried in Dayton, Washington, his reputation as the sole survivor of the battle at the Little Big Horn probably would have been buried with him if it hadn't been for his second wife. His story was largely a local one, accepted by most people who knew him for his habitual honesty. As long as Frank's buddies from Dayton were alive, nobody doubted the story in Southeastern Washington. Not much was known outside the state of Washington and nearby Idaho, where Frank's son Ben farmed and served 12 years in the Idaho state legislature. It would come to pass, though, that the Finkel survivor story would live on in encompassing areas and beyond, through the efforts of a woman driven by the need for recognition. The recognition was not to happen in the manner she hoped for, but the story survived with ironic twists worthy of a novel of the time.

The Depression was worsening, property values were plummeting and the Finkel family and in-laws were moving away. Life in Dayton held little for Hermie, just the memories of the man who was locally believed and honored as the survivor of the battle at the Little

Courtesy of Milton Koch

Frank in the late 1900s

Big Horn. But memories did not provide income. The memories, in fact, may not have been entirely happy. For several years of his marriage to Hermie, Frank had lived in a little shack of a house on his wheat land in Montana and left her in Dayton for months on end, though they never formally separated or divorced.[1] She may have changed his life a little too much for his own comfort. It seems he never forgot Delia.

But Hermie was a survivor too. She had learned survival as a single woman in Edwardian times when a woman was expected to be married. Undoubtedly she was a lonely woman after losing Frank's company, the affection of her step-children after her rather insensitive handling of Frank's last will and testament, and the attention that the reflected glory of the Custer survivor brought. In 1933, Hermie married a man named Henry M. Billmeyer and moved to his home in Oshkosh, Wisconsin that same year. There is no record of how Hermie, of Dayton, Washington, met Henry of Oshkosh, Wisconsin, with half a nation between their homes.

Henry Billmeyer was a recent widower who sold real estate and insurance while his wife Caroline had been a confectioner. They had a

Frank out in his cornfields

storefront shop located at 1006 South Main Street.[2] When Hermie settled in with her new husband, she took over the candy shop. She would also go on to take over something else, the renewal of Frank Finkel's reputation as the one and only Custer survivor.

While Frank was alive, Hermie had enjoyed the reflected glory of being the wife of a survivor of the battle at the Little Big Horn. When he passed away, she took on the role of the widow of the sole survivor of the battle. When she married Henry, she had no intention of giving that role up. Henry, apparently, a complacent man, signed on for the duration.

When Hermie arrived in Oshkosh she delved into the case by visiting local groups for talk-fests and the local museum for support. Keeping the flame alive and burning became increasingly important to her as things got worse in Oshkosh. This she could do, she knew, by gaining official recognition through the granting of a widow's pension by the U.S. Government. A pension, too, in the financial severity of the depression, would be welcome. Henry's businesses, real estate and insurance, had bottomed out and the neighborhood confectionary shop could only provide so much income. Hermie was a survivor, she would move forward.

When she formulated her plans for what would become an on-going frontal assault against the fortress that was the Washington bureaucracy, Hermie realized she might be up against an invisible wall. Thus would begin the first ironic twist and turn that would keep alive the Frank Finkel name and the Custer legacy and, importantly, fan a woman's obsession with reflected fame.

When Hermie Sperry Finkel Billmeyer decided to submit a pension request to the U.S. Government, she was facing a far different United States for German-Americans and people with German-sounding names than the Victorian America outfitting its troopers with Prussian helmets, the era when Frank (August) Finckle joined the 7th Cavalry.

Hermie's marriage to Frank Finkel occurred just a few years after the Treaty of Versailles, the treaty that placed the sole guilt for the Great War on Germany. The First World War sent 70 million people in most of the industrialized world into a conflagration that resulted in 15,000,000 fatalities and a level of emotional disruption rarely seen before. The United States had joined Britain, France, Belgium, Japan, and Italy against Germany and the Austro-Hungarian Empire—Russia dropped out just as America came in. The Great War cost the United States 112,000 American dead, the worst carnage in American history except for the Civil War of Frank Finkel's childhood. The Great War had come and gone and brought with it a total change of attitude toward German-Americans. During the War everyone was just plain American and if you were of German extraction, or even had a German-sounding name, it was a very difficult time.

When the United States entered World War I, Woodrow Wilson set up a commission called the Committee on Public Information (CPI), an organization headed by George Creel. The CPI emerged into a full-fledged propaganda organization with the purpose of directing the American people into supporting the war effort. Taking a cue from the British who had been in the business of war propaganda for three lurid years, the CPI developed an expertise in demonizing the Germans. Exerting its influence on all the media including Hollywood, newspapers, public speakers dispatched to communities across the nation, and even such innocuous publications as *The Ladies Home Journal,* the CPI steered the attitude toward the Germans into a 180 degree change.[3]

Anti-German Propaganda

German soldiers were falsely depicted as being savages. Stories of the bayoneting of babies for sport, chopping off their hands, and holding the little bayoneted bodies up as trophies, and the raping of women and cutting off of breasts were widely circulated, carefully calculated to raise the hate levels in America.[4] The mass shooting of Belgian military stragglers and civilian marksmen who fired on German troops from ambush—with some innocent hostages mixed in—was treated as an attempt to exterminate the entire population[5] Mass rapes of women and girls was described as endemic.[6] To add revulsion to the American emotional make-up, stories such as reports of eye gouging and the filling of a tub with eyeballs was added to the mix.

Life was not easy for German-Americans once patriotic America went to war. The dachshund was renamed the *liberty dog*, the speaking of German in many schools was banned, the playing of Beethoven was forbidden. Even the sick bed was included, with rubella being renamed *German measles:* the disease was falsely attributed to a Berlin laboratory that created it to cripple American babies.

Anti-German Propaganda

The Germans were even blamed by some for the influenza outbreak in 1918 and 1919, the first pandemic since the Black Death.

The levels of hate rose to frightening levels and individual incidents of intolerance were sure to follow. German-American homes were smeared with yellow paint, the color of cowardice. Shop windows with German names were broken. People with German surnames changed names to something less German-sounding. A public flogging of a German-American was reported in Florida, and across the land threats of tar and feathers and public execution were made against American citizens of German extraction unless they made public demonstrations of loyalty. Public humiliations were commonplace and one lynching actually occurred in Illinois. A German-American named Robert Prager smiled too broadly when he flunked his pre-induction physical for poor eyesight. His neighbors hanged him from a railroad trestle and his terrified parents buried Prager wrapped in an American flag to prove their own loyalty. Hate of everything German was everywhere. [7]

The human being is easily conditioned when the emotions are manipulated. When the manipulations cease, the emotions do not necessarily readjust. Hate, perhaps the most base of human emotions, bides its time. And when the hate is collective, those who are the object of that hate know fear. The CPI did nothing to readjust those emotions when the War ended in 1918.

Hermie Sperry was of Canadian origin and witness to the emotional disorientation that hate fosters. She wanted to be known as the wife, and later the widow, of the prosperous and respected Custer survivor from Ohio named Frank Finkel, not as the widow of a man with the more German-sounding August Finckle, who gave his birthplace as "Berlin, Prussia," when he joined the Army as a vagabond son of German immigrants in 1872.

It is not unreasonable to suspect that Hermie might have been more comfortable with a name less German-sounding than Finkel. She injected a new name into a litany of interviews to the press which added to a growing list of inaccuracies. She claimed that Frank Finkel had actually enlisted under the more Anglo-Saxon-sounding name Frank Hall. Her palpable yearning to distance herself from all things German would create a dust cloud of confusion and diversion for those researching the Custer survivor tradition.

The dust cloud first arose when Hermie decided that the one true way to get official recognition was by the granting of a pension by the Department of the Army to which a widow of a veteran of the United States Army was entitled.

When Hermie submitted the pension request, she knew first hand, more than most Americans, what hate meant. Being a Canadian national she had been aware of the force-feeding of German hate given Canadians by the British Bureau of Propaganda for three years before the American dose was rendered by the CPI. She had to know that Washington D.C. was where the decision to grant the pension would be made and, undoubtedly, the home base for the wartime anti-German propaganda. She would be understandably apprehensive about decision-making eyes looking favorably on the pension request for someone named August Finckle. She was bound to hit the obstacle that prejudice usually builds, the invisible wall. Hermie would do an end run. The name "Frank Hall" would lead the way.

THE UNITED STATES OF AMERICA.

OATH OF ENLISTMENT AND ALLEGIANCE.

State of _Kentucky_ } ss:

Town of _Louisville_

I, _Frank H. Hall_, born in _Syracuse_, in the State of _New York_, and by occupation a _Clerk_ DO HEREBY ACKNOWLEDGE to have voluntarily enlisted this _Fourteenth_ day of _December_, 1872, as a SOLDIER in the ARMY OF THE UNITED STATES OF AMERICA, for the period of FIVE YEARS, unless sooner discharged by proper authority: And do also agree to accept from the United States such bounty, pay, rations, and clothing as are or may be established by law. And I do solemnly swear, that I am _Thirty four_ years and _____ months of age, and know of no impediment to my serving honestly and faithfully as a Soldier for five years under this enlistment contract with the United States. And I, _Frank H. Hall_ do also solemnly swear, that I will bear true faith and allegiance to the UNITED STATES OF AMERICA, and that I will serve them honestly and faithfully against all their enemies or opposers whomsoever; and that I will observe and obey the orders of the President of the United States, and the orders of the officers appointed over me, according to the Rules and Articles of War.

Frank H. Hall (SEAL)

Subscribed and duly sworn to before me, this _14th_ day of _December_, A. D. 1872

_____

1st Lieut 3rd Cavalry

Recruiting Officer.

I CERTIFY, ON HONOR, that I have carefully examined the above-named recruit, agreeably to the General Regulations of the Army, and that, in my opinion, he is free from all bodily defects and mental infirmity which would, in any way, disqualify him from performing the duties of a soldier.

_____

Asst Surgeon

Examining Officer.

I CERTIFY, ON HONOR, that I have minutely inspected the above-named recruit, _Frank H Hall_, previously to his enlistment, and that he was entirely sober when enlisted; that, to the best of my judgment and belief, he is of lawful age; and that I have accepted and enlisted him into the service of the United States under this contract of enlistment as duly qualified to perform the duties of an able-bodied soldier, and, in doing so, have strictly observed the Regulations which govern the Recruiting Service. This soldier has _Gray_ eyes, _brown_ hair, _fair_ complexion, is _5_ feet _6 3/4_ inches high.

_____ (SEAL)

Frank Hall's Enlistment Papers

DECLARATION OF RECRUIT.

I, _Frank H Hall_ , desiring to ENLIST in the ARMY OF THE UNITED STATES, for the term of FIVE YEARS, DO DECLARE that I have neither wife nor child; that I have never been discharged from the United States Service on account of disability, or by sentence of a court martial, or by order before the expiration of term of enlistment; and that I am of the legal age to enlist of my own accord, and believe myself to be physically qualified to perform the duties of an able-bodied soldier.

GIVEN at _Louisville Ky_ this _14th_ day of _Decmbr_ , 187-2.

WITNESS:

A R Barker   _Frank H Hall_

Saml Sergeant

DIRECTIONS.

Enlistments must, in all cases, be taken in triplicate. The recruiting officer will send one copy to the Adjutant General with his monthly reports, a second to the depot at the time the recruits are sent there. In cases of soldiers re-enlisted in regiment, or of regimental recruits, the third copy of the enlistment will be sent as directed to regimental headquarters for the one.

Received A. G. O.

Assigned to the ____ Regiment of ____ U.S. Army.

Received of ____

Discharged ____ Reg't of ____ 18__

enlistment; last served in Company ( )

Enlisted at _Louisville Ky_ on the _14th_ day of _December_, 187-2 by _1st Lieut DePrera_ F... Regiment of _Cavalry_

No.

Frank H Hall

#227/009

CONSENT IN CASE OF MINOR.

I, ____ , DO CERTIFY that I am the ____ of ____ ; that the said ____ is ____ years of age; and I do hereby freely give my CONSENT to his enlisting as a SOLDIER in the ARMY OF THE UNITED STATES for the period of FIVE YEARS.

GIVEN at ____ the ____ day of ____

WITNESS:

Frank Hall's Enlistment Papers

DECLARATION OF RECRUIT.

I, _Frank H Hall_____, desiring to ENLIST in the ARMY OF THE UNITED STATES, for the term of FIVE YEARS, DO DECLARE that I have neither wife nor child; that I have never been discharged from the United States Service on account of disability, or by sentence of a court martial, or by order before the expiration of term of enlistment; and that I am of the legal age to enlist of my own accord, and believe myself to be physically qualified to perform the duties of an able-bodied soldier.

GIVEN at _Louisville Ky_____ this _14th_ day of _December_ 187_2_.

WITNESS:

A E Barker   _Frank H. Hall_

11 _Laur Sargant_

DIRECTIONS.

Enlistments must, in all cases, be taken in triplicate. The recruiting officer will retain one copy, and forward the Adjutant-General of the Army, a second, to the superintendent of the recruiting service, and a third to the depot at the time the recruits are sent there. In cases of soldiers re-enlisted in a regiment, or of regimental recruits, the third copy of the enlistment will be sent in like case to regimental headquarters for file.

Discharged _____ 18___

_____ Reg't of _____

_____ enlistment; last served in Company ( )

by _____

_____ Regiment of _Cavalry_

Enlisted at _Louisville Ky_ on the _14th_ day of _December_, 187_2_

No.

CONSENT IN CASE OF MINOR.

I, _____, DO CERTIFY that I am the _____

of _____; that the said _____ is _____

years of age; and I do hereby freely give my CONSENT to his enlisting as a SOLDIER in the ARMY OF THE UNITED STATES for the period of FIVE YEARS.

GIVEN at _____

the _____ day of _____

WITNESS:

Frank Hall's Enlistment Papers

The Hall Quandry, Frank and Others

One fabrication leads to another when the fabricator attempts to cover his or her tracks. The result is usually confusion. When Hermie fabricated the name Frank Hall she seemingly attempted to get around the invisible wall by changing the name under which Frank Finkel had enlisted, almost certainly because of the emotional discomfort generated during the Great War by the Wilson Administration working in conjunction with the British Propaganda Office. When she locked herself into the story that Frank had enlisted under the Anglo-Saxon-sounding name of Frank Hall, and not that of "August Finckle" of Berlin, Prussia—Frank's only recorded lie, except for his age—she covered the Custer survivor's tracks so thoroughly that neither the Army nor the experts that investigated could possibly take her case seriously. How she decided on the name *Frank Hall* is not a matter of record but it is not a far stretch from Frank Finkel. Frank's name change was the first of a series of "story changes" generated by Hermie as time progressed which served to confuse those researching for possible survivors of Custer's Last Stand. She had created a dust cloud rivaling anything the Sioux might have used in their battle forays.

Ironically, however, there actually was a man named Frank Hall in the 7th Cavalry but the only Frank Hall of the 7th Cavalry bore no resemblance to the recorded description of August Finckle. Frank Hall was five-foot-six-and-three-quarter inches tall with brown hair and gray eyes, about one-half-foot shorter than the description on the enlistment form of August Finckle—no mirror image of the six-foot Finkel.[8] He was born in Syracuse, New York and joined the Army in Louisville, Kentucky at the age of 34 in 1872 which would have made him 38 at the Little Big Horn. Nothing in Syracuse-born Frank Hall's enlistment file would explain how he was able to converse in German as well as he did in English, as attested to by Charles Windolph, Frank Finkle's Prussian-born best friend and by Hermie herself.

To add further dust to Hermie's fabrication, two other soldiers named Hall were on the 7th Cavalry roster in June of 1876, Edward Hall and John Curtis Hall. Both Halls, though, were accounted for alive after the battle. Edward Hall was on detached duty and not present at the Little Big Horn and John Curtis Hall survived on Reno Hill along with Kanipe and Windolph and lived until 1908. Neither Edward Hall nor John Curtis Hall was a casualty, nor a possible fugitive survivor.

Ironically and conversely to Hermie's contention, a Sergeant Frank Finkle does appears on the roster just below General Custer, Captain Custer, Sergeant Bobo, and Sergeant Finley. The second ironic twist that would confront Hermie would be the invisible wall she would create for herself. She was about to embark on a quest to find a man named Frank Hall who never was. The man, ironically, she created was an utterly impossible survivor candidate. Her pension request would die an early death.

But Hermie was a woman of resolve with an obsessive drive. Her husband Henry was disinclined or did not have the temerity to call a halt to her crusade. She never let up on her campaign to have Frank recognized as a veteran of the 7th Cavalry and a participant of Custer's Last Stand—and to be recognized herself, as the true widow of the sole survivor of Custer's Last Stand.

Hermie kept at it with a letter assault on official Washington for 10 years, until 1937. The file ended when Brigadier General Frank G. Burnett led the force that finally stopped the assault. The Acting Adjutant General, he told the Winnebago County Service Officer, William H. Miller, that there was no paper trail for Frank Finkel or Frank Hall.

> "I have your letter of September 2, 1937, with which you inclosed (*sic*) the application of Mrs. Hermie C. Billmeyer for a certificate in lieu of lost or destroyed discharge certificate for service alleged to have been rendered by Frank Finkel, alias Frank Hall, in Troop C., 7th United States Cavalry, under General Custer.
>
> "The name Frank Hall or Frank Finkel has not been found on the record of enlistments in the Regular Army for the month of September, 1874,

The Register of Enlistments records that Frank Hall deserted in May of 1875.

Company C

1st Sergeant
Edwin Bobo
Sergeants
Joseph Boerger
George August Finckle
Jeremiah Finley
Richard P. Hanley
Daniel A. Knipe
Edwin Miller
Corporals
William Brandle
Charles A. Crandall
Morris Farrar
John Foley
Henry E. French
Trumpeters
William Kramer
John Lewis
Farrier
John Fitzgerald
Wagoner
Frank Stark
Saddler
George Howell

Blacksmith
John King
Privates
Fred E. Allan
Herbert Arnold
James C. Bennett
John Brennan
John Brightfield
Thomas J. Bucknell
John Corcoran
Christopher Criddle
George Eiseman
Frank Ellison
Gustave Engle
James Farrand
Isaac Fowler
Patrick Griffin
James Hathersall
John Jordan
William Kane
John Mahoney
Frederick Meier
August Meyer
Martin Mullin

Thomas McCreedy
John McGuire
Ottocar Nitsche
Charles M. Orr
Edgar Phillips
John Rauter
Edward Rix
James H. Russell
Daniel Ryan
Ludwick St. John
Samuel Shade
Jeremiah Shea
Nathan Short
Ignatz Stungwitz
Alpheus Stuart
John Thadus
Peter Thompson
Garrett Van Allen
Oscar T. Warner
James Watson
Alfred Whittaker
Willis B. Wright
Henry Wyman

The Roll for Company C

nor has either name been found on the rolls of Troop
C, 7th United States Cavalry, from 1874 to 1879.

"The case of Frank Finkel has been before this
Department since 1927, and repeated searches of the
records have failed to identify the service alleged.[9]

This unaltering attempt, singularly focused, was centered, and
foundered, on her attempt to show that Finkel had enlisted under the
name of Frank Hall.

At some subsequent point, perhaps anxieties controlling her, alternatively, she later fixed on the name "Charlic Vaughn," pulled, perhaps, from desperation or fantasy, and not found on the 7th Cavalry
roster. In 1931 she hired a researcher to search the Washington files
and out the name "Charlie Vaughn" along with "Frank Hall." The researcher, Mrs. John A. Shirley, wrote back from Washington D.C. on
March of 1932 to tell Hermie it was a wild goose chase under either
of those names:

> "I found no Frank Finkel on the muster rolls,
> nor any one by the name of Frank Hall, nor of
> Charlie Vaughn. There is no record of enlistment of
> Frank Hall, Frank Finkel, nor Charlie Vaughn dur-
> ing the year 1874 nor in the years near that time.[10]
>
> "There was one August Finkel (sic) with Custer
> at the time of the last fight. He was killed. He was
> born in Berlin, Prussia, occupation clerk, age 27 at
> the time of enlistment, eyes gray, hair dark, dark
> complexion. Enlisted January, 1872 at Chicago."
>
> "There were other men by the name of Hall
> and Finkle, Finckel, enlisted at various times but no
> Frank and none of them enlisted at Council Bluffs
> nor whose age corresponded with that of Mr. Finkel.
> I find that men frequently get their dates of enlist-
> ment wrong, even tho they remember distinctly all
> that may have transpired during the period of their

enlistment. If you can give me any clue as to some other name, perhaps he used his middle name, I might try again. There were many young men enlisted under assumed names on account of their age. Where did the parents live at the time he enlisted.

"My fee for the research is one dollar. I make this price because I did not notify you and ascertain whether you wanted me to do the work. If this is not satisfactory you need not pay it. This work is interesting and I enjoyed it. I looked thru the rolls of all the troops engaged in this fight. Am sorry the records did not disclose any thing of Mr. Frank Finkel's record.

I am,
Respectfully yours,
Mrs. John A. Shirley

Dead Mail. The Ultimate Irony

Hermie's relentless quest to have Frank Finkel identified as a member of the United States Army, and subsequently a participant and the sole survivor of Custer's five companies at the Little Big Horn, had been ongoing for 17 years when a touch of irony worthy of a Victorian novel was added to her story. A government clerk trying to follow up on a pension attempt from her using the physical description of Frank Finkel, accessed August Finckle's file in the Old Military Records section of the National Archives in Washington D.C.

The folder on Sergeant August Finckle included the 1948 application to the Adjutant General for a pension from Hermie Billmeyer giving the description of her late husband: six-foot height, "blue" eyes and dark haired.[11]

The clerk had found only one match: August Finckle and Frank Finkel. The anonymous clerk could see what Hermie could not—or would not.

PAGE SIX

Frank Finkel Was Custer Survivor

Pioneer Leaves Story of Thrilling Escape From Indians.

The recent death of Frank Finkel, pioneer Dayton resident, makes of more than passing interest, the statement made public by Mr. Finkel some years ago regarding his escape from the Indians, as the only survivor of the Custer massacre, in 1874. Mrs. Finkel has recently written to the widow of General Custer, Mrs. Elizabeth B. Custer, 71 Park avenue, New York City, setting forth Mr. Finkel's claims to be know as the only survivor of the Custer massacre, but has not yet had a reply. The address of Mrs. Custer was secured through a friend of the Finkel family who lives in New York. Mr. Finkel left a written statement of his experience.

A brief review of Mr. Finkel's experience is as follows:

The men were trapped like rats, surrounded on all sides by Indians, and at the height of the battle Mr. Finkel was wounded, and almost immediately after a bullet struck his horse in the flank, causing it to bolt. As the horse ran through the Indians, a bullet struck Mr. Finkel in the side and another in the foot. His horse was sufficiently fleet to outdistance Indians who followed him for some distance. After nightfall he stopped by a stream and was lying in the grass covered with blood, his horse standing by him, when two Indians came by. They would have passed on in the dark, but Mr. Finkel's horse whinnied at their horses and they stopped. Thinking Finkel dead, or fatally wounded, they kicked him and then turned away to take his horse. As they turned he pulled his revolver and shot one of the Indians dead. The other, thinking he was in an ambush fled. He then took the ammunition belt from the dead Indian's body, mounted his horse and rode on in the night, fearing other Indians would come that way. He found another stream, but it was alkali. A prairie hen was sitting on some eggs near the water and he shot her and tried to eat the raw meat, but it made him sick. On the morning of the fourth day out, he came to a stream of fresh water. The wound in his side was giving him trouble by this time and the injured foot and leg had turned black. He reached a hut where a man was cutting wood, and after some difficulty convinced the man,

who kept him covered with a gun, that he was severely injured and needed help. The man finally helped him into the house, where another man lay ill of consumption. They did what they could for the injured man, even to probing with an improvised probe for the bullet in his side. They were unable to locate it. It came out near the naval some nine years ago, when it caused an abscess.

The foot was causing a great deal of trouble, and the men wanted to amputate it with a saw, believing it the only way to save the soldier's life, but Mr. Finkel refused to allow this. The men then fixed a syrup from pine pitch and poured it, boiling hot, into the wound. This treatment seared the wound and it healed. The wound in the side was treated with bear grease.

The consumptive died within a few weeks and Mr. Finkel remained with the other man until his foot got so that he could walk fairly well, when he decided to move on. The man with whom he had been staying agreed to show him the way to Fort Benton. At the fort he told his story and asked to be discharged from the army. He had no credentials and no witnesses, however, and the officers refused to issue a discharge. As a result he never received his discharge. He went to St. Louis, where he stayed for some time and later came west to Dayton and had resided in Columbia county for 51 years at the time of his death.

His story is a most interesting one, and it is unfortunate that he could not have secured his discharge, thus establishing with the government his identity as the one survivor of the Custer massacre.

MAN WHO ESCAPED IN CUSTER MASSACRE DIES

St. Paul, Minn.—(P)—Charles H. Low, 79, retired engineer of the Great Northern railway, who escaped death in the Custer massacre, died Friday at his St. Francis hotel home here.

Low, an army mule driver at the time, missed fulfilling an assignment to accompany Custer by the stubbornness of his mules.

From 1886, until his retirement some 12 years ago, Low was an engineer.

Union Bulletin articles

Why did Hermie react so fixedly regarding the Frank Hall name? She was almost certainly conditioned by the anti-German propaganda of World War I. When she first saw the description of August Finckle, she must have known he was the same person and frantically covered his tracks to make sure nobody linked her prosperous and respected husband to the man who gave "Berlin, Prussia," as his birth place in 1872. Hermie Sperry may have been more afraid of "Berlin, Prussia," than Frank Finckle had been, since he appears to have mentioned his name on the 1876 casualty list quite freely before his son Ben got into politics in Idaho.[12]

•

Hermie's obsessive search for verification of Frank Finkel's identity as the sole survivor of Custer's Last Stand resulted in a maze-like trail of contradictory fabrications and mistakes which have diverted many serious researchers from establishing the reality of Frank Finkel as the legitimate sole Army survivor at the Little Big Horn. Her constant trail of fabrications in areas other than the "Frank Hall" fixation included new stories about his enlistment, new sites where he did so, his underage status, his rank other than sergeant.[13]

She moved far away from the Frank Finkel of Dayton, Washington, the man who had pointed out his own name on the roster as "Finckle"—the same spelling he used when he married Delia at Dayton in 1886. She may have considered it good protection against suspicion that the late Frank Finkel was a Prussian officer or German sympathizer. Perhaps it was something else.

Hermie, who had taken possession of Frank Finkel's estate, however diminished it was, sought to take possession of his legacy, donning the mantle of widowhood despite the fact that she was married to another man. Her possessive nature reached out to the past to diminish the role Frank's wife of 36 happy years played by insisting that Finkel's first wife knew nothing of him being at the Little Big Horn battle. The implication was that by Delia's "lack of knowledge" about Frank being at the Little Big Horn, she was somehow a faded figure of the past and that, Hermie, Finkel's wife of just three years—

Billings Gazette

SECOND SECTION

BILLINGS, MONTANA, SUNDAY, JUNE 22, 1947

uster Massacre Credits Story of Soldier'

Inconsistencies Remain In Study of Endless Battle Survivor Question

By KATHRYN WRIGHT

Between the "Jaws of Hell," where white slabs mark the death of hundreds, and a single, rough-carved, secret stone lies the escape route of one who purportedly fled the holocaust of Custer's men.

The pathway, taken blindly by a wounded trooper when his maddened horse plunged through a mass of screeching savages, was "never charted. For this was the battle, according to historians, from which none who followed the golden-haired boy general returned.

None but Private Frank Finkel.

Not until Finkel's second wife, now Mrs. H. C. Billmeyer of Oshkosh, Wis., began a correspondence with Dr. Charles Kuhlman, a Polytechnic was the trooper's claim of survival held to the cold light of analysis.

After study of the story, Dr. Kuhlman, an authority on the Custer battle, said: "I believe Finkel participated in the fight and escaped from the battlefield."

Frank Finkel was a noncommunicative person with the quiet independence of a man determined to do the job at hand, little carring whether his wife was the result of an Indian's aim or a rusty nail in the barnyard of his Dayton, Wash., farm.

'Indian Shot Me'

His first wife had once asked the cause of his lameness and Finkel with characteristic directness said:

"An Indian shot me."

"Ah, go on," she had laughed. With a shrug he resumed his chores,

the subject closed until one day his second wife, now Mrs. Billmeyer, came upon a clipping in an attic trunk in the Dayton farm home.

The clipping was from the Walla Walla, Wash., Bulletin and contained a picture of Finkel and a brief account of his experiences as one of the region's pioneers.

Questioned about the clipping, Finkel told his story. He had enlisted in the Seventh cavalry in October 1874 under the assumed name, Frank Hall. He was very young for soldiering and he took the name because he had run away from home and was afraid discovery of his identity would lead to his return to the family farm.

From Council Bluffs, Iowa, where he enlisted, "Hall" was sent to the military post at Cheyenne, Wyo. This was far enough from home to lessen the runaway's fears. He dropped the assumed name and became Finkel, tallest trooper in the regiment that marched in fame and glory of past Indian wars to the grassy rolling hills along the Little Big Horn river, site of the most decisive defeat ever suffered by a United States military force.

According to the story Finkel told his wife, the battle preceding that defeat was at its height when he was wounded. He was with a line of C troops, still mounted and fighting on a ridge south of the hill where Custer was engaged. The ridge faced the river across from the underestimated Indian camp.

Alive With Warriors

The area between the ridge and the river was alive with warriors, their bodies making a solid stream of molten copper as gullies and ravines belched forth endless waves of redskins.

"We were trapped like rats," Finkel said.

He 'Lived to Tell' Battle Story

How he fled the Custer holocaust was told by Frank Finkel, right, to his second wife, now Mrs. H. C. Billmeyer of Oshkosh, Wis., left. Finkel, who died in 1930, farmed in Dayton, Wash., where the above picture was taken, then later operated a wheat ranch in northern Montana.

He raised his carbine to fire into an oncoming horde when a bullet struck the stock of his firearm. A splinter flew into his forehead. Blood gushed into his eyes.

Another bullet grazed his horse, sending the animal into wild gyrations. Finkel tried to wipe the blood from his eyes and lost control of his horse.

Freed from restraint the maddened roan reared, wheeled and plunged through a line of Sioux encircling the troopers on the south. Finkel flattened his body over the animal's back and hung on in a wild ride through the milling cavalrymen and Indians battling to the death.

A bullet struck him in the side; another tore through his right foot as three Indians gave chase.

The roan outdistanced the Indians' ponies, and with a parting shot the warriors turned back to the melee on the hill.

After putting more distance between himself and the battleground Finkel got a grip on the dangling reins, stopped his horse, slipped off into the prairie grass exhausted.

Blood from his forehead wound was congealed, but his shattered foot was still spurting. Tearing a strip from the saddle blanket, he fashioned a rude tourniquet, then remounted the roan and rode on dazed, weak and thirsty to the point of delirium.

It had been late afternoon when he escaped the battle. Now purple twilight was blackening into night. Still he pushed on, driven by thirst. Then—in the bottom of a coulee was the glitter of water.

Sliding from his saddle, Finkel threw himself face down on the bank. His mouth strained for the water.

It was alkali.

He lay vomiting into the grass. Nearby the roan nuzzled the earth for precious moisture. Then its head lifted, nostrils flared. A whinny sounded into the night as two riders approached.

Billings Gazette article

THE OSHKOSH NORTHWESTERN, FRIDAY, AUGUST 6, 1937

Oshkosh Woman Says Former Husband Was Massacre Survivor

Mrs. Henry Billmeyer, 1006 South Main street, a resident of Oshkosh since 1933, read with much interest the recent news stories in The Northwestern, containing information about General Custer's last stand against the Indians, June 25, 1876.

She persued the story from Washington, D. C., printed Tuesday, which told of an old diary written by one of the soldiers who died in the massacre, and she found pleasure, also, in reading Supt. C. C. Bishop's report of his visit to the famous battlefield, published Wednesday.

Hers was more than a casual interest, for in her possession she has newspaper clippings which bear out a claim which—to all indications—contradicts what history says of the battle.

History says that there was no white soldier who survived; the accepted version is that Custer and all of his men died in that "last stand" against a superior force of Indians.

Mrs. Billmeyer firmly believes that Frank Finkel, her former husband, now deceased, fought in that battle, and "lived to tell about it" because his wounded horse dashed frantically through the Indian lines and carried him out of reach of pursuers.

BELIEVES STORY TRUE

Could this be true? History says otherwise, maintaining that Custer's entire force was wiped out. Mrs. Billmeyer is certain that Frank Finkel told the truth. He had a reputation for honesty, and his story was believed without question by residents of Dayton, Wash., where he lived after his army service and where he died in 1930.

Before he died, Frank Finkel told his story to interviewers, and appeared as speaker at a Kiwanis meeting. His facts were always the same; he never bragged or exaggerated on what he considered was his "true" story.

Those who knew Frank Finkel readily believed his claim that he was the lone survivor of the Custer massacre, but beyond that there has been no official proof. However, there are certain developments which, indirectly at least, give support to the Finkel story. Among these are:

Rain-in-the-Face, Red Cloud and Crazy Horse, Indian chiefs who fought in the battle, in statements at various times, all asserted that one trooper, severely wounded, got through their lines. This corresponds to Finkel's story. Was he the man?

The American Legion magazine of April 1927 printed a story of the west, including a description of Custer's battle, in which an In-

dian participant was quoted: "One enlisted man on a white horse escaped . . . this trooper somehow managed to ride through the encircling attackers and dash up the stream." He was pursued for a distance, and the chase abandoned. The Indians were of the opinion he committed suicide later, believing that capture was inevitable.

ADMITTED BY INDIANS

It seems to be a common agreement, among Indian historians, that a white man escaped through their lines, but there is no information as to what happened to him afterward.

Frank Finkel could not prove his story with official records, for several reasons: He had enlisted under age, and therefore had to use an assumed name "Frank Hall." Army records have not contained information to support the story.

Frank Finkel never received his army discharge. He asked for it when he got to Fort Benton, some time after the battle, and was denied it because he could not produce two witnesses, to attest his service in the army. Those who knew him in the army were dead.

He was close-mouthed about his adventure, and the story might never have come out, except one time he interrupted a debate about Custer's battle, giving an opinion of his own. Somebody asked, "What do you know about it?" and he replied, "I was there." That remark led to further inquiry and drew the story from him.

Finkel's first wife never knew the story. He never told her. The story might also have escaped notice of his second wife, now Mrs. Billmeyer, except that she discovered an old clipping which told of his participation in the battle, as had been told years ago in the debate. She inquired about the story, and gained the full information.

RAN AWAY FROM HOME

Frank Finkel and a chum ran away from home in Ohio, according to the story, and enlisted in the army. Finkel was in Custer's organization sent to the plains to fight the Indians.

In the height of the battle, a bullet struck the butt of his gun, sending a splinter of wood against his forehead, just over the eyes, cutting a deep gash. The blood flowed into his eyes and nearly blinded him. He carried that scar in later years, and called attention to it when he told his story of what happened.

At almost the same moment he was hurt, another bullet struck his horse in the flank, making the animal frantic with pain. The

horse galloped wildly away, and there was nothing fo. Frank Finkel to do but to bend low and hang on.

As he rode through the ranks of the Indians, he was struck twice by bullets. One of them smashed one of his feet, creating an injury that crippled his foot permanently. The other bullet struck him in the side, and progressed through his body, finally lodging in his abdomen. This bullet, Mrs. Billmeyer said, was removed in later years, when its irritation bothered him.

OUTDISTANCE_ INDIANS

The Indians chased him, but his fright-crazed horse outdistance pursuers, and he was able to reach the hills and go into hiding. He made a tourniquet out of a blanket to stop the flow of blood. After hiding for four days, with practically no food and no water, the escaped trooper approached a cabin in the woods.

When he asked for aid, he was curtly refused, and told to be on his way. He pleaded he was so weak he could not go on, and as he slumped in the saddle, the cabin occupant came forward with a gun to investigate. Mr. Finkel said he was helped into the hut, where there was another man in bed, ill.

The man in bed gave instructions on how to treat the wound in Mr. Finkel's foot, and when all other methods failed, the flow of blood was stopped by pouring hot pitch on the open sore. The two men in the cabin were uncommunicative. They told nothing about themselves, but the armed man was called "Bill."

Here is another angle of mystery for the story: Were these men trappers, or were they outlaws hiding out? Mr. Finkel never found out. He was permitted to stay there to recuperate. When he was nearly well, and could hobble about, the man in the other bed died. Mr. Finkel and the remaining occupant dug a grave on a knoll.

CARVED INITIALS ON STONE

Desiring to honor the dead, Mr. Finkel suggested that they erect a cross. He asked the dead man's name, and the companion replied, "It's none of your damned business!" They finally compromised when the man said the initials were "G. W." Mr. Finkel laboriously carved these initials on a stone, and placed that as a marker.

Mrs. Billmeyer hopes that some day some one will report the finding of a stone in Montana, with the initials "G. W." on it. She feels such a discovery would be proof of an important part of Mr. Finkel's story.

Later Mr. Finkel, guided in the right direction by "Bill," set out for Fort Benton. He boarded a boat bound downriver, and when he reached Bismarck, N. D., he saw a newspaper, and learned for the first time that Custer's soldiers had been wiped out in the battle, and that it was considered no one survived.

He went to St. Louis, and then proceeded west to Dayton, Wash.,

where he lived for 50 years. He was considered one of the pioneers of that community, honored and respected by all.

Oshkosh Northwestern article

the wife he left behind for endless field trips to Montana—was the true Custer survivor widow.

Hermie had a working relationship with the staff at the Oshkosh Public Museum where she arranged for an ongoing file to be opened to house the newspaper clippings and letters received relative to the ongoing Frank Finkel inquiry she was conducting.

One of her techniques for reshaping the past was to add addendums to existing papers.

In a typescript addendum to Frank Finkel's self-written piece in the *History of Southeastern Washington* published in 1905, Hermie withdrew Delia from the account completely. Hermie's typescript omitted any reference to Delia or Finkel's three living and two deceased children from his marriage to Delia, along with his political and club memberships. "The balance of the article referred to Mr. Finkel's first marriage, his children, political affiliations, etc, Have not copied that (p)art of the article, as it has no bearing on his personal life or character."[14]

The failure to be inclusive in the recounting of Frank's life is an indication of the selective memory on Hermie's part. She chose to write, or believe, whatever would further the satisfaction of her obsession—the subjective belief that her three years of marriage to Frank overshadowed his 36 years and five children with Delia.

Interestingly, Hermie always got his actual American birthplace right. It was the one consistent element in her confused collection of names and places.[15] Interestingly also, the maze of misinformation she created lived past her and continued to reinforce the myth of no survivors at the battle of the Little Big Horn. The final irony is that it is the maze of misinformation that kept the Frank Finkel story an open option to this date, an option that is positively concluded in this, the 21st Century, 134 years after that eventful day in the Valley of the Little Big Horn River.

Notes

[1]Milton Koch, Frank Finkel's great-grandson, told the author that Frank would live by himself in Montana for months at a time, leaving Hermie in Dayton. The family had no idea how she later met Henry Billmeyer.

[2]Oshkosh Public Museum Director Brad Larson provided some useful background on Hermie Sperry and Henry Billmeyer.

[3]Knightly, Phillip, *The First Casualty*, Johns Hopkins Press, 2002, reprint 1975 edition.

[4]*Ibid*. Phillip Knightly reports that when the stories of hand-lopping and mutilated children were examined after the war, in the 1920s, not a single instance was ever substantiated. The stories still turn up today, mostly in propaganda. Ironically, the Belgians themselves sometimes lopped the hands off African children during the days of the Congo Free State circa 1900 to force the adults to work harder. This torture was sometimes photographed and widely reported and provoked protests in Britain, the United States—and Germany.

[5]Strachan, Hew, *The First World War,* Simon & Schuster. 2003, pages 48-53. Strachan substantiates shootings of Belgian adults as snipers, but describes the rapes and mutilations as sheer British propaganda. He notes that the British also fabricated the shootings of priests and nuns, which never happened either.

[6]Wolff, Leon, *In Flanders Fields,* Times Inc. Book Division, 1963 reprint of 1958 original by Viking Press, page 85. French peasant mothers of blond German-fathered babies in areas recaptured by the British were honest enough to deny they had been raped: 'They had no need to use violence in their love-making. There were many volunteers.' They rubbed their thumbs and fingers together as though touching money and said 'You understand.?' German propagandists, conversely, told their own civil populations to expect rape by dark-skinned colonial troops in the French and British armies if Germany lost the war.

[7]*The Grolier Library Of World War I,* Vol. 5, esp. pages 62-63. The conductor of the Boston Philharmonic, Karl Muck, was also arrested and interned when he refused to play "The Star-Spangled Banner."

[8]National Archives of the United States, file on Frank Hall, 7th Cavalry, 1872-1875. Hall was listed as a deserter in May of 1875, a year before Custer set out for the Little Big Horn and not seen afterward.

[9]Oshkosh Public Museum, letter from the Adjutant General of the United States to Mrs. Hermie Billmeyer in 1937.

[10]*Ibid*, letter from Mrs. John A. Shirley to Mrs. Hermie Billmeyer.

[11]*Ibid*, letter from the Custer National Battlefield Monument to Mrs. Hermie Billmeyer.

[12]*Ibid*, stories about Frank Finkel from the Union Bulletin of April 8, 1920 and March 20, 1921 based on actual interviews with Frank and not Hermie. He said on March 20 that he was the man on the roster—Second Sergeant George August Finckle of C Company—and never used the name Frank Hall.

[13]*Ibid*, Hermie's first story, undated but probably about 1930, says that Finkel enlisted with a "chum" at Omaha, Nebraska, when he was about 20. She says he enlisted under the name of "Frank Hall" because he

did not want his parents to know he was in the Army. In the *Oshkosh Northwestern* of August 6, 1937, Hermie has Finkel running away from home in Ohio "with a chum" and enlisting while under age, as Frank Hall, with no location of enlistment provided. By 1938, in an article in the *Oshkosh Northwestern* of February 16, Hermie has him enlisting under the name of Frank Hall in Council Bluffs, Iowa, in 1874. She also says that he was immediately sent to the battle of the Little Big Horn, which she says also took place in 1874—instead of June 25, 1876. In the *Billings Gazette* of June 22, 1947, she has him enlisting under age in 1874 and being sent to Cheyenne Wyoming—while the 7th Cavalry was stationed at Fort Abraham Lincoln in Dakota Territory in 1874. Her wanderings have three consistant facts: Frank came from Ohio, Delia never knew his story, and wherever he enlisted, it wasn't Chicago…where "August Finckle" joined the Army in January of 1872 and signed with Frank Finkel's handwriting.

[14] *Ibid*, Hermie's retyped transcript of the 1905 *History of Southeastern Washington* pointedly omits Delia Rainwater Finkel and Frank's three living and two deceased children. Since everybody in Dayton knew about Frank's survivor status and the story had been published twice in newspapers, her confabulation is obvious and extreme. In one version of the confabulated saga, in the *Oshkosh Northwestern* of Friday, August 6, 1937, a reporter who interviewed Hermie was to write: "Finkel's first wife never knew the story. He never told her. The story might have escaped notice of his second wife, now Mrs. Billmeyer, except that she discovered an old clipping which told of his participation in the battle … she inquired about the story and gained the full information." Ten years later, the "old clipping" had been found in an attic trunk, according to Hermie, and Delia had scoffed at the story and shown no interest when Frank told her he had been shot by an Indian as reported in the *Billings Gazette* of Sunday, June 22, 1947.

[15] Hermie's wild confabulations about where Finkel enlisted and what his age was are compounded by serious lapses of memory—*Walla Walla Union Bulletin*—Hermie's letter from Oshkosh to Washington state written some time after 1933 says that one of the "fugitive desperadoes" "died of wounds he carried." The other accounts all say G.W. died of tuberculosis. But Frank's birthplace on Ohio remains absolutely consistent—probably because his relatives still lived there.

Chapter Eleven

The Naysayer

Psychological studies of human behavior opened up at the turn of the twentieth century when Freud and Jung started looking at the mindsets of the Victorian era. Since then the understanding of the human mind and subsequent behavior patterns has advanced considerably. The manner in which humans learn is of particular pertinence in the determination of Frank Finkel as a survivor of the Little Big Horn. Conversely, it pours a beam of light on why he wasn't previously determined as such.

Psychologists hold that most human beings, some holding that as many as 95 percent, learn by imitating and accepting as true what is told by others who they view as authorities, or, by what is popularly agreed as being true. This is because of convenience, the need to learn quickly in a culture with a super-abundance of new material is important, but it often leads to a failure to analyze all the facts emotion-free, before making a decision.[1]

The perpetuation of myth is based on the acceptance of popularly believed fact by people who, without analysis of fact, pass on to others their beliefs. The myth that George Armstrong Custer died

with his gallant five companies "to the last man" was accepted as true
because of the religious-like fervor that fueled the belief at anniversary events, in literature and in film, and were reinforced at other such
happenings. The Custer Myth had the ring of romanticism, generous
sacrifice, total love of nation. There was no need to analyze the facts,
limited as they were. It would be inconvenient to do so. It might even
be un-American. Defenders of the myth were quick to leap to the
parapets. One such stalwart was Christian Madsen, a self-proclaimed
Little Big Horn "expert" who fired off a quick defense of the myth
when he received a letter of inquiry posing the possibility that could
puncture the swollen balloon of myth.

The letters came from Arthur P. Kannenberg,[2] a curator of
the Oshkosh Public Museum. After the United States Army denied Frank's recognition as a veteran or survivor, Hermie turned to
Kannenberg for help. She had ingratiated herself to the museum per-
sonnel and she was developing a Custer Survivor file.

Madsen was a former Regular Army soldier rising to first sergeant, and a law officer for 25 years after his Army discharge. A crusty
character by any description, he was a genuine frontiersman, famous
as one of the "Three Guardsmen" who cleaned up the Oklahoma
Territory. Madsen had served as a U.S. Deputy Marshal for many
years, both before and after his last military assignment as the quar-
termaster sergeant of Teddy Roosevelt's Rough Riders during the
Spanish-American War of 1898. His credentials, excellent in many
regards, were hardly ones for a determination of the validity of Frank
Finkel's presence and survival at Custer's ring of death.

As a U.S. Deputy Marshal for 25 years on either side of the
Spanish-American War, and as a veteran of three five-year hitches
in the U.S. Army before that, Madsen had heard his share of Custer
Survivor yarns, and they apparently formed a negative predisposition
in his mind regarding Custer survivors. Madsen, over time, came to
represent all the negative arguments against the reality of a Custer
Survivor.

"On account of my connection with the
Government in different capacities, soldier, peace
officer, investigator, superintendent of a Soldier's

Home for nearly 62 years, my name has been known to (a) great many people and I have had so many inquiries about the facts in cases like this one. Some time there is a reason for the inquiries but reason alone cannot always make facts, and even to-day I have a request about Custer, who some persons claim to have met and recognized somewhere in the Black Hills lately.

Another, a tramp riding or leading a burro, came to the Soldier's Home while I was superintendent of the institution and told a pitiful story about having been thrown and hurt, and begged to be admitted to the hospital. After I got talking to him and let him tell his story to have been with Custer as a scout at the time Custer was killed, but had got away and hid in the brush near the river from where he saw Custer's body floating down the stream. He also told about having married an Indian Princess and that she and he had been riding with Custer on his trips. That was enough and after an examination by the doctor, who found no marks of any kind to indicate that he had been hurt, I told him what I thought of him and made him leave the Home. And that is only one of many incidents where some fellows have been trying to deceive the people to obtain something for nothing."[3]

Credentials firmly established, he then went on answering Hermie's letter which Kannenberg had sent him:

"I am sorry to inform you that the statements made by you ... set forth a possibility which under the circumstances could not have existed for the following reasons ...." "Had your husband enlisted under any name mentioned by you, his name would have appeared on the Muster and Pay Roll of the company at the end of April 1876, whether he was with the company or on detached duty. If he was a member of the company on June 25, 1876, the time of the fight on the Little Big Horn, his name would also have appeared on the roll of June 30th, whether dead or alive.

"Whether his name was Finkle or Finkel is of no importance, as there was a Sergeant Finkle serving in the company, and had been for four years before the massacre, and he was one of those killed. The first report of the fight was given by the *Bismarck Tribune* on July 6th, 1876, a copy of which I have, and the name there is spelled Finkle.

"The total number of killed and wounded (for C Company) was only 42, and as the company must have been at least 50 strong there would have been some man left who could have identified him had he returned to his company for his discharge. In fact had he returned there, he would have been sent to the hospital for treatment or held as a deserter. Some men from the company were evidently absent either on detached duty or guards with the supplies. And as only two Sergeants were killed it is also certain that four others, the regular number in a company were not there, and could easily have identified any member of the company if he returned to the company. And the company records, which were not destroyed, would also have been sufficient proof of his membership in the company. "

"Now as to your husband hanging on to his frantic horse for a distance beyond the area occupied by the Indians, and him bleeding from three wounds, and then remaining in hiding without food for four days, and then mounted his horse again. And approached some cabin, and there met some occupants who took care of him for a while, do you believe that a man who had three bullet wounds would have been able to mount a frantic horse, with the loss of blood stopped only by a torn blanket? He would have been so stiff and sore that (he) could not have moved, if he had even been alive, and do you believe that hot pitch would have stopped the blood several days after he had been wounded (?). It would more likely have blistered him to such an extent that he never would have been able to move."

"The fact that the man claimed to be a person enlisted under the name of Hall, had run away from home and on that account had enlisted under a fictitious name points to some reason why he did not have a clean record behind him, and farther that he had kept his real identity from his first wife, and left her in ignorance of his military experience, also seems to point to a belief that he did not desire to have his past life enquired into."

"The story about the White Horse (*escaping from the battle*) is the same as has been told by numerous other men who in the past claimed to be 'the only ones' who escaped from Custer's battle, and Crazy Horse nor Sitting Bull never made such stories to any reliable writer. I am acquainted with the man who went to Sitting Bull's people for the story of his life. There is nothing in the story about any white horse; in fact Sitting Bull was not in the fight much himself—he was the medicine man, well behind the lines. And Crazy Horse surrendered shortly after the fight and was later killed by a soldier at Fort Robinson and in 1935 when a monument was unveiled at that place for him, and all his kinsfolk were there, I was one of these invited to be there, and talked to them about the old chief, but not a word was said about any white man escaping at the fight at the Little Big Horn."

Madsen knew the old Army and his life's experiences left their marks as they do in all human beings. He came down on the Frank Finkel claim like a sledgehammer on an anvil for a reason that is palpable, if not commendable. Like so many human beings, when he came to his decision, he fell within the 95 per cent parameter. He didn't consider all the facts and the emotional factor may have played. The overlooked facts were abundant:

- Frank Finkle was obviously in no mood to be held as a deserter, which, technically, he was, and he was so badly hurt that he was immobilized for weeks afterwards. By the time he recovered, he had obviously decided he'd had enough Indian fighting. Madsen is correct in saying that the records were enough to establish his identity, and would have if Hermie hadn't clung to the Frank Hall fantasy and had honestly admitted that Finkel was Finckle.

- Madsen neglected to mention that Captain Frederick Benteen and other officers noticed that C Company had fragmented,

- that few C Company horses were found on the battlefield,

- that C Company's Lieutenant Henry Harrington had completely disappeared,

- that C Company's Corporal John Foley could have escaped if he hadn't panicked and opted for suicide,

- that C Company's Trooper Nathan Short's body was found 25 miles from the battlefield. All these fugitives who almost made it were intensely relevant to the story of the one fugitive who had actually made his escape.

A fact to be considered in Christian Madsen's perspective on matters pertaining to Prussia, and things and possibly people Prussian, was that he was born in Denmark, just north of Germany.

Prussia, August Finckle's purported birthplace, had made its military reputation by beating up on three of the armies Madsen had served in. He was a 14-year-old messenger boy in the Danish Army in the Second Schleswig War of 1864, a Foreign Legionnaire fighting for France against Prussia in the Franco-Prussian War of 1870, "at the battle of Sedan, September 1 and 2, was twice wounded and taken prisoner but then escaped"—and a *garibaldino* fighting for the French Third Republic in the last phase of the Franco-Prussian War with Giuseppe Garibaldi and his sons. Garibaldi and sons trounced some Bavarians. The Prussians then rode to the rescue and trounced Garibaldi, though the Prussian generals said he was the worthiest adversary they had ever fought. Madsen lost his three wars with Prussia and had the scars to prove it.

Denmark, his homeland, lost a large chunk of territory. He had good reason not to like Prussians, real or bogus. He actually volunteered for another crack at the Germans in World War I but was rejected because he was pushing 70.

That may explain why an otherwise shrewd and lucid old man, 87 years of age when he answered several of Hermie's letters, also failed to include all the known facts. Many soldiers on Reno Hill were shot, some more than once, with .44 Henry or Winchester bullets and lived. And the land east of the Little Big Horn and the Yellowstone country was a known hang-out for outlaws and drifters. But Madsen's negative dismissal on the Frank Finkel story focused almost entirely on Hermie's fabrications and mistakes, not on the story Frank Finkel told his horseshoe neighbors and the Kiwanis in Dayton.

The failure to include all the facts by Christian Madsen is obvious. It was typical for the time. It was difficult to assemble all the facts, the information was not easily available; and people often make decisions when driven by emotion.

•

One positive development that emerged from the Madsen experience for Hermie was that she found out that Sergeant Charles

Windolph, who won the Congressional Medal of Honor at Reno Hill providing covering fire for the water relief party, remembered Frank Finkel. He had gone back to find his body, and couldn't locate it—an excellent confirmation.

(After Frank, Hermie, and Windolph were all dead, Windolph passing in 1950, and Hermie in November of 1951, critics of the Finckle story circulated untrue reports that Frank Finkel had been offered the chance to meet Windolph and had backed out, a definite falsehood. Windolph didn't learn of Finckle's purported survival until long after Finkel was dead, and said he would have loved to meet his old friend, whom he still believed was a former Prussian officer before joining the 7th Cavalry: "He was a gallant soldier."

When he was shown an old photograph taken of Finkel in 1921, when Finkel would have been 66, Windolph, who was 93 by the time he saw the photograph, said that his eyes were so bad that he couldn't tell whether the gray-haired man resembled his 22-year-old dark-haired friend or not. The height should have been ample confirmation, since no other enlisted man in the 7th Cavalry had been over six feet tall.

Hermie, whose pattern of diminishing anyone connected to Frank Finkel before her marriage to him, wrote condescendingly, almost dismissively, of Windolph as having had something to do with the battle, instead of describing him as a hero of Reno Hill and a Medal of Honor winner, which would have been factually accurate and more generous in sharing whatever glory Custer left to anybody else at the Little Big Horn. She may not have known all the facts about Windolph's Congressional Medal of Honor for covering the water party from Reno Hill. Or she may not have cared since she wanted all the glory for her husband.

Notes
(1)*Influence: The Psychology of Persuasion*, Robert B. Cialdini, PhD. William Morrow and Company.
(2)Finkel File, Oshkosh Public Museum, letters to Arthur Kannenberg and Hermie Billmeyer from Christian Madsen, all mailed in 1937.
(3)Arthur P. Kannenberg was involved with the Museum at the Oshkosh Public Library and was an early member of the Board of Directors of the Oshkosh Public Museum in 1923. He served as president from

1928-1933. He also served on the Board of the Winnebago County Archeological and Historical Society. He was a self-educated archeologist and was awarded the Lapham Medal for meritorious work in archeology in 1935. He was president of the Wisconsin Archeological Society and held the position of Curator of Archeology at the Oshkosh Public Museum from 1935 until his death on March 1, 1945.

Chapter Twelve

The Champion

A failure to assess all the facts was not a trait ascribed to just the self-styled experts. It also showed up in a highly-educated Custer expert who did believe Frank Finkel was a survivor. Ironically, it was for the wrong reason.

Dr. Charles Kuhlman, a retired college professor with a doctorate in European history from the University of Zurich and the first Custer expert with serious academic credits, was also the first *bonafide* expert to seriously consider Frank Finkel as a possible survivor. Kuhlman, born in 1872 in Nebraska to parents who had been born in Prussia and spoke German at home, was bilingual just as Frank Finkel was. He terminated a satisfactory academic career teaching European History at the University of Nebraska when he went deaf in late middle-age. Occurring concurrently to the death of his wife, it left him depressed and listless until he discovered the Little Big Horn battlefield and was mysteriously revitalized. [1]

Kuhlman roamed the battlefield from end to end, endlessly, until he knew the ravines and hills as if they were his own backyard or family burial plot. He sometimes used the odometers of three different makes of automobiles to measure distances and he took sightings at the exact hour and on the exact day of the year to determine just what any of the senior officers could have seen at critical moments of the battle.

Kuhlman's central theme was that Custer had been betrayed by the cowardice of Marcus Reno and, perhaps, the malice of Frederick Benteen, whom he felt may have dawdled on his way to reinforce the five companies at the Little Big Horn.

Custer was Kuhlman's hero, a Prussian love for authority comes through in all his work, yet he was not unsympathetic to the Indians: "…they knew from bitter experience that cavalry in an Indian village made a frightful mess of things, destroying tepees and other property, killing ponies, women, children and old men. It is well to remember these things when studying the Battle of the Little Big Horn." [2]

Kuhlman believed that Custer could have been saved if Captain Benteen had been more active in coming to his aid, and if Major Reno had been less of a coward. This conclusion, following the discovery of the number of repeating rifles the Indians used at the battlefield, is somewhat subjective and dated. Many of the older accounts depict the Indians as fighting with bows and arrows and old muskets, not Henrys and Spencers and Winchesters. The volume of fire from the Sioux and Cheyenne probably would have turned any serious rescue attempt from Reno Hill into a total extermination of the 7th Cavalry. One officer who was actually there said that if the survivors hadn't been commanded by a coward, they would have all been dead.

Kuhlman was initially offended by the very notion that there might have been a Custer survivor. He had encountered a number of patently fake stories on his own and read others in the files of Earl Alonzo Brininstool, a former investigative reporter from New York and New Jersey, a Custer-hater and the ultimate Survivor Skeptic.

"The number of self-proclaimed escapees from the action on Custer Field is legion," Kuhlman wrote in 1949. "The character of the tales they have told 'would make a graven image smile'—or weep. It is not at all strange, therefore, that whenever a new aspirant for the distinction of 'sole survivor' appears, the student of the battle should feel an irresistible impulse to swing his arms and give forth strange noises. Along one line or another, all of us, sooner of later, reach our limit, and then we pull the cord of the safety-valve to forestall a cerebral hemorrhage." [3]

Kuhlman said he hadn't seen Brininstool's entire collection of 70 "sole survivor" stories, but he had picked up a few of his own while conducting his meticulous topographic survey of the battlefield, "I have not read this priceless collection, but have come across a few myself," Kuhlman wrote. "Among them was one containing the following gem. This 'survivor', who shall remain nameless, said that he was mining gold at Rosebud, when Custer marched up and without so much as a 'by your leave, sir,' virtually confiscated him and set him to work to carry letters to Mrs. Custer and bring back her replies. So, from that time on he was kept busy carrying letters back and forth. He did not say what means of travel he employed, but he must have used a supersonic rocket, or something faster, for Custer started up the Rosebud at noon on the 22nd and was killed on the Little Big Horn around six o'clock on the 25th. It is quite a trek from Fort Lincoln, North Dakota, near Bismarck. It took Custer from May 17 to June 21st to cover the distance, with only a few days out while camped on Powder River. If my memory serves I left this 'survivor's' story at item twenty-four of falsehoods and crude misconceptions." [4]

The Kannenberg Connection

After finding disappointment with Christian Madsen, Arthur Kannenberg found Dr. Kuhlman, who subsequently found in his mailbox the Billmeyer report, Frank Hall present and accounted for.

After studying the information provided him, Dr. Kuhlman's eyes may have widened as he studied the terrain over which the Survivor rode his horse because of his meticulous analysis of the terrain, he knew that Finkel's description of his escape ride fit perfectly into the topography.

Tracing Finkel's escape on the wounded horse from what he knew of the break-up of C Company, Kuhlman noted that Finkel would have ridden through a fire zone that was tactically clear of

Indians for about 300 yards: the Indians couldn't swarm into this zone because the angle of the terrain would have exposed them to long-range Springfield fire from higher ground. The anonymous trooper who hit Lame White Man right in the heart just as the Cheyenne war chief shouted: "Come on! Now we can kill them all!" shows that Kuhlman was also accurate. Finkel could have ridden down the hill under Indian fire but wouldn't have been body-blocked by Indians. He would have ridden over their bodies as long as the troopers kept up their fire.

Kuhlman's Three Streams of Water

The three branches of water that Finkel described would have been Tullock's Creek, located between the Little Big Horn and the confluence of the Rosebud and the Yellowstone, where the dead C Company horse was found in August of 1876. Two of these branches, Kuhlman wrote, would have been contaminated by alkali in 1876, but the third branch would have probably been sweet due to the patterns of vegetation in the days before over-grazing. "It should be explained here that in this region these small creeks may be dry, or nearly so, one day and roaring torrents the next, or anything else in between," Kuhlman wrote in a 26 page pamphlet in 1949. "The middle branch of the Tullock's (is) about six miles east of the battlefield, as measured by the speedometer of a Chrysler sedan over the Crow Agency-Busby Road.

"Nearly all such creeks, including Reno Creek, are dry today, or nearly so, most of the time because of over-grazing on the range land years ago. The stock, especially sheep, leave little standing above ground, hence there is no dead vegetation to check the run-off during heavy rains. The effect of this is to turn small creeks and ravines into torrents within a few minutes of a heavy downpour. This is followed by a subsidence almost as rapid as the rise.

"This was not true in 1876. The creeks did not rise so fast because the rains sank into the soil more, and were slowly fed into the stream so that, except during prolonged dry periods, there was usually some water in them. Then, it is quite probable that during the extremely wet summer of 1876, when torrential rains began the second week in

May, there probably was some water in the small creeks. Finkel may have found some in Ash Creek, the middle branch of Tullock's, also in one of the eastern tributaries—all within eight miles of Custer Field. The good water to which he finally came was, without doubt, a short, eastern branch that comes into consideration here. It comes right out of the high bluffs bordering the valley of Tullock's here.

"From the high bluffs where I viewed it, it seemed to me that it originated in an alkali flat. This, of course, is a mere guess, but it is supported by the fact that it is bordered along its course as far as I could see by trees which do not spring up along streams heavy with alkali. There are no trees along the course of Ash Creek, or the middle branch of Tullock's, as far as my vision carries.

"Along the east branch there is a good growth of pines along its whole course down to the valley. If Finkel's story is true in detail, here is the place to look for the grave of 'Bill's' pal. The outlaws, if such they were, would not have located on an alkali stream, nor would anyone else have done so for that matter. Aside from this, the rough ground and the timber made a good hideout from which they could watch the valley below without being seen themselves.

"To sum up, the Finkel story does not contain any of the usual marks of fraud," Kuhlman said. "He might never have told of his experience had he not been 'off guard' in the good old country sport of 'pitching horseshoes' one Sunday afternoon. His companions happened to get into an argument about the Custer battle and they evidently had some ideas about it that were probably at variance with the facts—nothing unusual, be it said—so much so that Finkel burst out with 'A hell of a lot you know about it.' Asked how *he* came to know anything about it, he replied, 'Well, I guess I know. I was there.'"[5]

Hard to Kill

Kuhlman pointed out that Finkel was "technically ... a deserter" and concluded that the story he told about trying to obtain his discharge papers in 1876 after his wounds and escape from the Little Big Horn was self-serving hokum.

"It is useless to speculate as to just what it was that led him finally to decide to neglect the formality of a discharge to clear his record," Kuhlman said. "It may be pointed out, however, that he was still young, had nothing that today could be called an 'education,' and had little imagination not concerned with the material things of the objective world. He was of the type called 'stolid' but not in the sense of being stupid. Far from it. Persons of his type do not cross bridges before they come to them and are usually hard to kill, by either physical or mental processes. They would not recognize a psychosis if it mistakenly hit them in the eye. A man as physically sound as was Mr. Finkel, but of a high-strung nervous type, might not have survived his experience. But there are many others who have passed through similar, or even worse, ordeals and have survived. His story, therefore, cannot be rejected on this score.

"Our conclusion, then is that there is nothing fantastic or unbelievable in the Finkel story," Kuhlman wrote in the 1949 booklet that had remained long unpublished. "Finkel could not possibly have known anything of what happened south of (Custer) Hill unless he had been in the fight himself, or had been present on the field. For there is not a chance in many millions that his account would have fitted so snugly into the facts if he had manufactured his story out of whole cloth. [6]

A Touch of Arrogance

Two things threw Kuhlman's endorsement slightly askew, despite his topographical confirmation that Finkel's escape was entirely possible. Kuhlman's emotions intruded. Shut off from the outer world by his deafness and his age, he retained the kind of German ethnic arrogance that had long since ceased to be fashionable in the days after the Nuremberg Laws and the Nuremberg War Crimes Trials. His conclusive reason for accepting Finkel's story set a lot of teeth on edge:

> "...considering his fiery independence evidenced throughout his entire life, and his type of Teutonic pride understood by every intelligent person of Germanic descent, it can be safely assumed that had a pension been offered to him on a gold

platter he would have scornfully refused it as constituting more or less of an insult …Take a look at the reproduced photograph (of Finkel and Hermie) and decide for yourself whether or not this man should or would have fabricated such a story either for money or cheap notoriety." [7]

Kuhlman's second flaw hinges on this first endorsement of unshakable Germanic rectitude: Finkel *did* fabricate at least two aspects of his life—he was born in Ohio, rather than "Berlin, Prussia," and he was 18 rather than 27 when he joined the Army in Chicago in 1872.

Overlooking the Facts

Charles Kuhlman, incredibly, didn't realize that August Finckle and Frank Finkel were one and the same person. Despite his training, not only in European history, but in agronomy and botany, Kuhlman never seems to have compared the height, eye color, hair color, ethnicity, and birth month of the August Finckle enlistment with the data he must have seen from the Custer National Battlefield Monument and with Hermie's description of Frank Finkel posing as Frank Hall when she tried to collect his pension in the 1930s. Hermie romanticized Finkel's eyes from "gray" to "blue"—the color shift happens all the time with pale eyes in any case, but the Army of the 1870s consistently recorded all pale-colored eyes as "gray" as a matter of policy. [8] The exceptional six-foot height and the hair color are forensically identical, and the spelling drift on the marriage and land records and handwritten signature on the probate of Delia's will confirm that the Finckle of the Little Big Horn was the Finkel of Dayton, Washington. It was a fact that Kuhlman never grasped. He was so confident that Finkel would never have told a lie, even as a scared teenaged vagabond, that he never realized just how firm the survivor story actually was.

Dr. Charles Kuhlman's fixation on Frank Finkel's oaken honesty as a middle-aged and older man caused him to overlook the fact of the perfect match, made by the clerk in the Dead Letter Office of the National Archives in 1948 between August Finckle and Frank Finkel: height, eye color, hair color, and bilingual ability. Surprisingly too, one other factor not given consideration by the scientific-minded Dr. Kuhlman, a comparison of the Frank Finkel and August Finckle signatures: handwriting analysis.

Notes

(1)Pohanka, Brian, in the introduction to the Stackpole edition of *Legend Into History* provides a multi-page biography of Dr. Charles Kuhlman.

(2)Kuhlman, Charles, *Legend Into History*, page 155. Like most serious and objective Custer scholars, including E. A. Brininstool, W.A. Graham, and especially David Humphrey Miller, Kuhlman was not hostile to Indians. Dr. Thomas Marquis and John G. Neihardt were emphatically pro-Indian.

(3)Oshkosh Public Museum, Finkle file. Kuhlman never paginated the common-domain essay he left to the Oshkosh Public Museum, with a spare copy at the Chester Fritz Library at the University of North Dakota. This comment appears on the first page.

(4)Kuhlman manuscript, page 1.

(5)*Ibid*, page 9.

(6)*Ibid*, page 7.

(7)*Ibid*, page 10.

(8)Research conducted over a dozen years at the National Archives by the author shows that the vast majority of soldiers in either the 41st New York Volunteer Infantry, a three-year German-speaking regiment in the Civil War, or the 7th Cavalry, are listed as having either "gray" or "brown" eyes. Variants such as "blue" or "green" are almost unknown.

Part Three

The Facts

Chapter Thirteen

The End Of Her Trail

Hermie Sperry Finkel Billmeyer had a strange role in the saga of the Custer Survivor. So eager to prove that her former husband was the only survivor of the Little Big Horn, she brought some of the details that were vital evidence in firm focus: the fact that Finkel had served in C Company and that he rode a sorrel roan were both keys to the conclusion that he broke out from the battle and escaped as he told the newspapers when he was still alive, and as she told everybody who would listen once he was dead.

But Hermie was impelled to one lie by her immense jealousy of Frank's first wife. Her blunt statement that Delia hadn't known anything about his military service made Frank himself sound like a liar, even though Delia clearly knew everything and so did everybody else in Dayton who could pick up a newspaper or gossip at the drug store. Hermie's immense fear of "Berlin, Prussia" on the enlistment form made her cling to the "Frank Hall" fabrication that enabled skeptics to make the whole case look ridiculous.

Hermie fooled a lot of people with her "Frank Hall" story, but in the end she only fooled herself. In November of 1951, having outlived her endlessly patient second husband, she fell at home at the age of 87, spent three weeks in an Oshkosh hospital, and died of coronary thrombosis.[1] She never got her pension. The final irony is that since Frank was technically a deserter, she couldn't have qualified for a pension.

Hermie kept the story of the Custer Survivor alive, through the dedicated help of Arthur Kannenberg and Charles Kuhlman—yet provided a stumbling block with "Frank Hall" that kept most people from believing it. Only forensic proof that couldn't be dismissed or denied as willful fantasy eventually showed that Frank Finkel was telling the truth—even if Hermie, his leading advocate, made things up as she went along so that most people didn't believe it.

Notes
[1]Department of Public Health, Oshkosh County, death certificate of Herminie Billmeyer, 1951.

Chapter Fourteen

They Almost Made It

The chaos of battle often provides unpredictable results. Those results are sometimes caused by the human instinct to preserve life but strong military training can often override that instinct. Discipline didn't work for a large part of the 7th Cavalry. The Richard Allan Fox finding in the 1980s confirms reports from some Reno Hill survivors that the 7th broke down as the Sioux and Cheyenne reacted to the attack with an enclosing envelopment of humanity and firepower. Chaos occurred almost immediately when the Sioux and Cheyenne reversed the momentum of the surprise attack. Some veteran officers and non-commissioned troopers stood their ground and fought with stubborn courage. Some troopers reacted to preserve life.

When C Company broke up under the hail of Indian gunfire and Lieutenant Harrington and the stunned and wounded Sergeant Finckle charged down Calhoun Ridge and through the Indians, they weren't alone. Six or seven other troopers rode with them, some of them probably wounded.

"One long sword escaped …." Rain-in-the-Face told W. Kent Thomas in 1894 when the crippled war chief and the white writer met at Coney Island. "His pony ran off with him and went past our lodges (at the foot of Calhoun Ridge) … I remembered hearing the squaws tell about it after the fight."[1]

Childless at 60, crippled in one leg, Rain-in-the-Face was a man with a solid reputation. His account of the Little Big Horn ridiculed the versions that had been offered to the public and jibed perfectly with the archaeology of the battlefield in the 1980s, which demonstrated that the Sioux and Cheyenne had fought with almost 200 repeating rifles and had Custer's weary men out-gunned by a factor of five or ten to one.

"We were better armed that the long swords, their guns wouldn't shoot but once, the thing (*ejector*) wouldn't throw out the empty cartridge shells …. When we found they could not shoot we saved our bullets by knocking the long swords over the head with our war clubs. It was just like killing sheep. Some of them got on their knees and begged; we spared none—ugh!"[2]

The Indians kept a careful count of their own dead, and they also kept a careful count of the troopers who got outside the circle of death and were killed by pursuing teenage Indians with no family concerns.

One trooper from C Company, reacting instinctively, was pursued by three young Indians. He had chevrons on his sleeves, probably Corporal John Foley, Irish-born, black-haired, bald, middle-aged, unable to read, eager to escape what he thought would be harrowing torture. The three teenagers, without rifles, had used up their last arrow and Foley's horse was gaining on them, when, to their amazement, he pulled out his Colt .45, pointed it to his own temple, and pulled the trigger. The three young Indians were astounded. They said that if the trooper hadn't killed himself, he would have escaped.[3]

First Sergeant James Butler of L Company, a soldier with 22 years of service, made it almost as far as Foley before he too was killed and left on the field, about half the distance between Foley and the bodies of C Company at Calhoun Ridge.

The ultimate fugitive, other than Finkel, was Private Nathan Short, the only man in C Company with a white hat or a bob-tailed sorrel. Short got about 25 miles and reached the Rosebud River before his horse collapsed and fell on him and both died together.

Short's body was found long afterward, his carbine still slung around his shoulder. The '7' pin on what was left of his white hat and markings on the carbine sling identified his skeletal remains.[4]

Lieutenant Henry Moore Harrington's body was never identified, though a skeleton found years afterward and miles from Calhoun Ridge with a steel trade arrowhead wedged in the backbone may have been his.[5]

The pro-Custer Crow Indians, enemies of the Lakota, said that they found six skeletons with 7th Cavalry equipment years later. These men had apparently been ridden down by pursuing Indians several miles from the battlefield and briefly held off their pursuers in a last stand after the Last Stand. Nobody in the Army even went out to look for them.[6]

"I saw human bones here and there, several miles away from the field," a white scout named Thomas Laforge wrote years later in his book *Memoirs of A White Crow Indian*. "I saw remnants of soldiers' bodies as far away as Rosebud Creek, 25 miles to the eastward. (This would have been Nathan Short.) Rotted-away clothing, articles and an occasional firearm or ammunition belt were scattered all about the region for 14 or 15 miles …. It was evident that many soldiers escaped from the immediate encirclement by the Sioux and Cheyenne, and it was also evident that they were pursued and killed, or some of them may have died of wounds and the hardship incident to solitary travel in this country."[7]

As many as eight or ten men may have escaped the immediate killing zone at the Little Big Horn. But all of them were pursued by the Indians and killed within hours afterwards or, in the case of Nathan Short, probably succumbed to injuries and died when his horse gave out and fell on him.

Only Frank Finkel, wounded and on a wounded horse, left the battlefield behind him and lived beyond June 25, 1876.

The Indians had kept the seven companies under Reno and Benteen pinned down on Reno Hill through the hideous night of the 25th and much of June 26th. Then they set fire to the grass to cover their withdrawal and left headed southward, band by band, family by family. "It was like some Biblical exodus; the Israelites moving into Egypt, a mighty tribe on the march," Windolph remembered.[8] The survivors on Reno Hill were relieved but they stayed on their bastion, surrounded by dead and wounded men and horses.

Those troopers who almost made it had reacted instinctively. There was another too, who reacted instinctively. Ginger, a sorrel roan, wounded in the flank, panicked and in an attempt to escape the sudden pain, galloped wildly, eastward, along the Little Big Horn River into the wilderness. Slumped in his saddle, blood streaming on his forehead, was a trooper with chevrons: the semi-conscious form of C Company's Second Sergeant, Frank Finkel.

Notes
[1]Brady, Cyrus Townsend *Indian Fights and Fighters,* page 291.
[2]*Ibid*, page 295.
[3]Hammer, Kenneth, based on Walter Camp's interviews, *Custer In '76,* page 199.
[4]*Ibid*, page 248.
[5]Connell, Evan S., *Son Of The Morning Star,* page 314.
[6]*Ibid*, page 312-313.
[7]Finkel File, Oshkosh Public Museum. Dr. Charles Kuhlman quoting Thomas La Fore in *Memoirs of a White Crow Indian,* as told to Dr. Thomas Marquis.
[8]Windolph. Charles, *I Fought With Custer,* page 106.

Chapter Fifteen

The Bravest Man and the Horse That Made It

There was one official survivor of Custer's five companies, but he couldn't tell his story, except by the sight of his harrowing wounds. Comanche, the claybank gelding ridden by Captain Myles Keogh, was found on the battlefield near the body of his owner, a man honored by the Indians as "the bravest of the brave."

Born in Limerick, Ireland in 1840, to a family of the Catholic gentry, Myles Keogh had studied at St. Patrick's College for two years, then taken ship for Italy where he served in the army of the Pope in the struggle for Italian unity. Captured by the Piedmontese, he accepted a parole and was decorated for his service with a Papal medal he wore around his neck for the rest of his life. Keogh honored his word to fight no more in Italy and took ship for America, joined the Union Army in the Civil War, and was cited for gallantry in dispatches more than once: "*Major Keogh, Aide de Camp to Major General Stoneman, went forward with a detachment of the 12th Kentucky Volunteer Cavalry. … surprised and routed the rebels near Salisbury,*

Courtesy of the Little Bighorn Battlefield Monument Museum

Myles Keogh in his Prussian-style dress uniform

killed 9 and captured 68.... Much credit is due to Major Keogh.[1] The Irish adventurer fought in 30 major battles and dozens of skirmishes without a scratch and finished the Civil War as a colonel. When the war ended, like Custer himself, Keogh took a demotion to stay in the smaller post-war Regular Army and spent most of his career in the 7th Cavalry.

Keogh missed the Battle of the Washita in 1868 because he was on staff duty, but at the Little Big Horn, though overshadowed by the Custer brothers, was commander of I Company and of one wing of Custer's five companies at the Little Big Horn. He was riding Comanche when an Indian bullet smashed through his left knee and toppled man and horse side by side. Still holding the reins, Keogh drew his sidearm and kept fighting despite agonizing pain: "Like the flame of a coal blazed his eyes. His teeth glistened like a fighting grizzly …," one Indian told a scout years later.[2] Keogh's courage was contagious and his sergeants and trumpeters rallied around him and fought it out while other soldiers panicked. They all died in a burst of gunfire but the Indians were so impressed with Keogh's defiant courage that they left his body intact when they stripped him to his socks. The Pope's medal was left untouched around his neck.

Comanche had been hit multiple times after the bullet that smashed Keogh's knee had dropped him in his tracks. The Indians left him on the field—either because he wasn't worth stealing in his wounded condition, or because, as some say, Keogh's dead hand was still clutching Comanche's reins when the Indians took his clothes but left his body uncut, and this was "big medicine"—or a very bad omen.

"And on the whole field where Custer and those four (*sic*) companies were wiped out not a living being was left to tell the tale," Sergeant Kanipe remembered. "One horse survived—his name was Comanche—when he was found he had seven bullet wounds. He was Captain Keogh's horse….

"They buried the dead and then began to carry the wounded, including the horse Comanche, to the *Far West* steamboat which had come up the river as far as it could. It then backed down the Yellowstone River.

"Most of the wounded got well, Old Comanche did, and there was an order from general headquarters that this (only) survivor of Custer's battle was to have a box stall for the rest of his life."[3]

Comanche was nursed back to health on a diet of bran mixed with whiskey, which gave him a lifelong taste for alcohol,[4] and he was given a personal orderly in the person of Trooper Gustav Korn, whose own horse had broken down during the charge for the Little Big Horn, and who turned back and joined the survivors on Reno Hill. The man and the horse bonded and Comanche transferred his affection from the gallant Myles Keogh to Gustav Korn, who had been Company I's farrier, the man in charge of shoeing horses, and who lived under a shadow since he hadn't died with the rest of Captain Keogh's I Company. The friendship lasted 14 years and Comanche was led, riderless, in dress parades of the 7th Cavalry.

Myles Keogh's horse Comanche, who famously survived the battle, with Pvt. Gustav Korn

When Trooper Korn was killed at the engagement at Wounded Knee in 1890, Comanche seemed to lose the will to live, and he died of colic in November of 1891. His body was preserved by the taxidermist's art and in 1893 he appeared at the Chicago Exhibition along with Rain-in-the-Face. Comanche is still on display at the Dyche Library of the University of Kansas.[5] The Indians ran off a number of other horses at the Little Big Horn, and the troopers and infantrymen put the crippled horses out of their misery, but Comanche, Myles Keogh's steed, remained the only official survivor of Custer's five companies for more than a century after the dust settled on the Little Big Horn.

Notes
[1]Connell, Evan S., *Son Of The Morning Star,* pages 290-294.
[2]*Ibid,* page 293.
[3]Graham, W.A., *The Custer Myth,* page 250.
[4]Barnett, Louise, *Touched By Fire,* page 328-329.
[5]Reedstrom, Ernest, *Bugles, Banners, And War Bonnets,* pages 229-231.

Chapter Sixteen

After the Battle

Looking for Frank Finkel

The aftermath of any battle is a particularly harrowing event. The sight of bloating bodies, often mutilated beyond recognition, was a common occurrence during the Indian Wars. The search for buddies would be particularly disturbing for the troopers of the 7th Cavalry with Marcus Reno.

On the morning of June 27, the soldiers trapped atop Reno Hill saw a handful of troopers and scouts headed their way. Giovanni Martini, the last white man to have seen Custer alive, sounded his bugle and the strangers rode in. General Terry's column of the 2nd Cavalry and 6th Infantry had arrived with the three Gatling guns and the Rodman cannon after the Indians in the valley had fled.

For the first time, the men on Reno Hill learned what had happened to Custer and his five companies. Exhausted, officers and men mounted their horses and headed downhill to find their buddies.

"Suddenly we caught a glimpse of white objects lying along a ridge that led northward," Charles Windolph, Frank Finkel's closest friend wrote. "We pulled up our horses. This was the battlefield. Here Custer's luck had finally run out."[1]

The naked bodies were scattered roughly where each of the five companies had been destroyed in detail, but Captain Benteen saw and said that a lot of bodies and most of the horses seemed to be missing from C Company, Finkel's company.

"Most of the troopers had been stripped of their clothing and scalped," Windolph said. "Some of them had been horribly mutilated …. I tried to find the body of my German friend, Trooper Finkle, the tallest man in the regiment. But I could not identify him."[2]

"I looked over the dead and recognized here and there a buddy and a sergeant that I knew," Sergeant Daniel Kanipe said in his final interview in 1924.[3] "I recognized Sergeants Finkle and Finley. Sergeant Finley lay at his horse's (Carlo's) head. He had 12 arrows through him. They had been lying there for two days in the sun, bloody and the wounded mutilated. You could tell what men had been wounded because the little Indians and the squaws would always, after taking the clothes off the men, shoot them full of arrows or chop them in their faces with tomahawks. They never hurt a dead man, just those that were wounded."

Here and there a man was spared. Myles Keogh was set aside as the "bravest of the brave" because of the fight he put up even after a bullet shattered his kneecap. Captain Keogh was stripped to his socks but untouched except for his death wounds. A medal he had received soldiering for Pope Pius IX was left around his neck.

Corporal William Teeman, an old soldier from Denmark who had befriended Rain-in-the-Face when Rain had been in the guardhouse a year before, was also largely unmolested.

"Everybody was scalped and otherwise mutilated, excepting General Custer and Corporal Tiemann (sic) whose scalp was partly off and who had the sleeve of his blouse with the chevron uplaid over it in a peculiar manner," a sergeant from the 6th Infantry wrote to the New York Herald for a story dated August 1, 1876. "This enabled a good many men of the 7th Cavalry to detect one of the participants in the fight on the Indians' side in the person of Rain-in-the-Face, who was in the guardhouse last winter and chained to a corporal, also a prisoner at the time."[4]

The butchery and the bloating of the corpses prompted one officer to commit suicide and many officers and men to seek early discharges. Major Reno and Captain Benteen drank themselves out of the army, and Captain Thomas Weir drank himself to death before the end of the year. Most of the dead on the hills above the Little Big Horn were so badly mutilated that, when they were discovered by General Terry's relief column two days later, they were impossible to identify correctly.

The numbers, however, tell the story: the count was originally 197 dead soldiers, later expanded to 210, but this left almost a dozen men from Custer's five companies unaccounted for: four men fell out with "horse troubles" on the ride down to the river and later rejoined Reno and Benteen on Reno Hill. Sergeant Butler and Corporal Foley were found two days after the battle and listed with the slain, but Private Short and the six men Laforge mentioned were left out of the body count at the Little Big Horn. Sergeant August Finckle was listed as dead on the field, obviously by mistake after Kanipe turned away in horror and disgust from whatever corpse he thought was Finkel.

The burial parties, such as they were, only added to the confusion. Rank had its privileges, even in death: the officers were buried in shallow graves, while the enlisted men were covered with sagebrush and rocks and left to the wolves and the crows. Finley and "Finkle" actually got marked graves, the only ones in C Company except for Tom Custer, who was found near his brother, beaten to a pulp by vengeful Indians. He had to be identified by initials tattooed on his hand, his face was battered beyond recognition.

A year later, the scattered bones of Companies C, L, E, I, and F were given a burial, and a few years after that, the bones of the horses, and some shattered bones of the men, were sealed in a block of cement. Most of the enlisted men were buried under markers that said "Unknown" and some men got two markers each, which led to constant confusion among experts who tried to examine the tactics of the battle. Identification became utterly impossible, especially since the men were stripped naked and no buttons or badges were left among the bones.

Three bodies turned up as late as the 1980s, including Mitch Bouyer, half French and half Lakota with a Crow wife, one of Custer's scouts, who had been missing since 1876, forensically identified be-

Charles Windolph at age 88. He lived another 12 years.
The star decoration is the Congressional Medal of Honor and
the round medal is the Indian Wars Medal.

cause of his mixed race, his age and the mark that his constant pipe
had grooved in his teeth.

Kanipe returned to farming in North Carolina and also worked
for the Internal Revenue Service, joined a social group called the
Mystic Tie Lodge #237, and served as a captain in the North
Carolina Militia Home Guard in World War I. He was active in
the Presbyterian Church. Rich at the end—his house was a virtual
mansion—Kanipe, who married First Sergeant Edwin Bobo's widow,
Missouri Anne Wyckoff, produced three birth sons and three daughters besides his two Bobo stepsons. He died in July of 1926. Despite
his mistake with the butchered corpse that he thought was Finkel,
Kanipe could have identified the living Frank Finkel easily—but died
before Hermie started her quest.[5]

Charles Windolph, the last white survivor of the 7th Cavalry
from Reno Hill, had won the Congressional Medal of Honor and

promotion to sergeant as one of four riflemen who provided covering fire for the water party who ran downhill, under fire from the
Indians, to bring back water for the wounded. Unaware that Finkel
had escaped, Windolph suffered pangs of remorse for the rest of his
life because he hadn't been able to give his best friend a decent burial.
Windolph retired from the Army as a first sergeant when he married.
He later worked as a harness maker and teamster, mostly in South
Dakota. As an old man, he moved in with his married daughter and
her husband in the town of Lead.

When Hermie Billmeyer finally contacted Windolph in 1944
through Dr. Arthur Kannenberg, her volunteer researcher, almost 15
years after Frank Finkel had died in 1930, Windolph, who was then
well past 90, had lost most of his eyesight. He said he couldn't honestly tell if a photograph of Finkel as an old man, provided by Hermie,
had been the dashing second sergeant of C Company or not.

The circulated story that Finkel had turned down a chance to
meet Windolph is untrue: neither man knew of the other's survival
during Finkel's lifetime and Windolph didn't know Finkel had survived until long after Finkel's death.

"After the battle Daddy says he looked everywhere for him—
as he was like a brother to him—but the bodies were so disfigured
that he was unable to find him ..." Windolph's daughter told Dr.
Kannenberg, who bribed the old soldier with chocolates, rationed
during World War II. "He has never forgotten him and has spoken
of him through all these years .... Dad said he came from Germany,
worked here for a couple of years and then joined the Army. Seeing
Daddy had run away from Germany when he was drafted into the
Army made this bond of friendship more binding between them."[6]

Notes
[1]Windolph, Charles, *I Fought With Custer,* page 110.
[2]*Ibid,* page 112.
[3]Graham, W.A., *The Custer Myth,* page 250.
[4]*Ibid,* page 357.
[5]Kanipe Family Web Site.
[6]Finkel File, letter from Mrs. G.C. Fehliman to Dr. Charles Kannenberg.

Chapter Seventeen

It's All in the Writing, the Final Fact

Witnesses for the Sergeant at the Little Big Horn

Two handwriting experts, a police forgery identification expert, a genealogist, and an archaic handwriting specialist bring together the evidence and the conclusion to the Frank Finkel saga that experts of yesteryear did not or could not do. Dr. Kuhlman, a neighbor to the battle site at the Little Big Horn and intrigued by its mystique and mythology brought considerable confirmation to the landscape of the story but failed to study all the facts.

Four people, removed by 133 years from the heat of the battle, bring the missing facts together and render a confirmation that one trooper, contrary to the mythology embracing the event, did escape that heat, and lived to tell about it. The facts are in the writing.

Frank Finkel or Finkle habitually let the Columbia Courthouse clerks sign off on his land transactions. Most of the signatures on the deeds that made him prosperous are not in his own handwriting. There is one significant exception: the signature on the probate of Delia's will, legally required so that the small fortune they built together could pass into his hands and his alone.

Two signatures from the 1872 enlistment form in Chicago. National Archives, Old Military Records.

Hasty signature in lead pencil from 1914. Courtesy of Milton Koch.

Two signatures from the probate of Delia' Finkel's will in 1921. Columbia County Courthouse, Dayton, Washington.

Signature from Frank Finkel's own will, three days before he died in 1930. Columbia County Courthouse, Dayton, Washington.

Signature of the real Frank Hall, who joined the Army in 1872, not 1874, and was five inches shorter and 12 years older than Frank Finkle. The real Frank Hall deserted a year before the Seventh Cavalry set out for the Sioux War of 1876 and was not carried on the roster or the casualty list. National Archives, Old Military Records.

The signatures in question

Finkel's 1921 signature on Delia's probate, matched against his 1872 signatures of the U.S. Army enlistment papers in Chicago, prove that he was the same person: there was no person "August Finckle," it was an alias for Frank Finkel—his spelling at the time invented him.

Objective analysis by trained experts confirms that by examining the 1872 and 1921 signatures, despite changes due to age and the coarse nib of the second pen, handwriting experts say the same man wrote both of them half a lifetime apart.

Dr. Thomas P. Lowry

"About the two Finckle signatures, done forty years apart," writes Thomas P. Lowry, MD, of Virginia, a retired USAF psychiatrist, medical school professor, and published author on the legal and medical aspects of the Civil War, "There are certain striking similarities, especially in the k."

"Certainly, there are dissimilarities: the cross-bar of the (*first*) F is new, and the initial ligature of the i is different.

"On the other hand, the angle of slant appears identical. The slight hesitation and arachnographia in the 1921 version is most likely due to increasing age.

"Overall, I would vote on a similarity sufficient to be the same man."

Dr. Lowry graduated with a medical degree from Stanford University where he studied both medicine and history. He served as a medical officer and psychiatrist in the U.S. Air Force, was a practicing psychiatrist for 35 years, and taught medicine on the faculty of the University of California at San Francisco. He specialized in Civil War medical and legal records and was the author of a dozen books on the Civil War era. One of his specialties, along with his knowledge of medical treatment and surgery in the 19th Century, was deciphering and analyzing handwriting—"there were no typewriters in Lincoln's day"—and his books include mainstream anatomical and psychiatric medical texts and Civil War and frontier history, published by university presses. His titles include *The Story the Soldiers Wouldn't Tell*, about sexual misconduct, *Tarnished Scalpels*, about medical malpractice, and *Tarnished Eagles*, a definite account of the courts-martial of Civil War colonels and lieutenant colonels. Dr. Lowry was perhaps the greatest authority in recent times on medical and psychiatric aspects of the Civil War, including the analysis of handwriting to determine identity, mental acuity, and level of education.

Chief John Ydo

John Ydo, police chief of Wyckoff, New Jersey, was a pre-med student in college before he vectored into police work and studied handwriting analysis at the John Jay School of Criminal Justice in New York City, with subsequent courses at the FBI Academy. Chief Ydo is regularly called on to provide forensic assistance in homicides and other serious crimes that require a knowledge of scientific technology as a member of the Bergen County Fatal Accident Squad. He speaks and reads Dutch as well as English and is familiar with European as well as Anglo-American penmanship.

"The comparison of the first sample signature, August Finckle, to the second sample signature, Frank Finkel, reveals unique similarities suggestive that both were written by the same individual," Chief Ydo wrote. "Specifically,

1. The cursive script is similar, in that it is straight rather than rounded in appearance.
2. The lettering slant is similar and within 4 degrees of one another.
3. The capital letter F is very similar and in both samples distinguishable by an additional and unique vertical appendage on the cross-line mid-letter.
4. The dotting of the i in both cases appears heavier than normal.
5. In both cases the letter k is very distinctive and similar. Noteworthy is the letter height and the inward appendage indenting the body of the letter.
6. Both styles are similar, of American origin rather than European.

Considering the totality of the above facts it is reasonable to assume both signatures were written by the same individual."

Chief Ydo confirmed that the handscript was the work of someone who learned penmanship in an American school and obviously not that of a Prussian officer or anyone else who learned penmanship in 19th century Germany.

Police Captain Keith Killion, Forgery Expert

Former Police Captain Keith Killion specializes in the legal aspects of handwriting and is expert at determining forgeries, and was frequently called on by the Police Department of Ridgewood, NJ to examine crimes involving forgeries.

"Once you explain the change in spelling and understand the age change, it's clearly the same person," Captain Killion said. "The F in the second name is distinctive and most of the other letters are almost identical. The change in size and neatness are what you expect with the aging process. I would go with it being the same guy 50 years apart."

Astrid Baker, Archaic Handwriting Expert

Astrid Baker, a reference librarian with a BS and an MS in Library Science from Rutgers University, was born and grew up in Baden, Germany, and attended German schools there before emigrating to the United States. Archaic handwriting of the 18th and 19th Centuries is one of her special interests.

"These appear to have been written by the same person," she said. "The F is German, but the uncial letters were written by an American. Nobody who attended a Prussian school would have written like this. The Prussian handwriting is so different that it's almost illegible—I have trouble reading Prussian script myself."

Sandra Luebking, Genealogist

Sandra Luebking, a professional genealogist, published author of three books on genealogy and editor of *Forum,* an international magazine for genealogical research, looked at the signatures from a slightly different perspective.

"A professional genealogist seeks to document the life of each individual within a kinship group. This research requires a record-by-record examination of all available evidence amassed over time. The difference in the two signatures in question would be resolved by (a) the full documentation of Frank Finkel from birth to death and (b) the proving or disproving of the existence of a second individual named August Finckle. Completion of these two steps would be the genealogist's determination as to whether or not the same person is represented in both documents.

"Although I am not qualified to assess specific handwriting similarities, I can say with certainty that instances of given and sur-name changes and spelling variations in 19th and 20th century iden-tifications is quite common. Therefore, fully expecting the research done by Mr. Koster is consistent with what I would do, in my opinion the variance in the signatures would not prevent a genealogist from concluding this could be the same person."

Ms. Luebing holds university degrees in history and anthropol-ogy from the University of Illinois and is a recognized researcher in heritance claims in the United States, the United Kingdom, Canada, Germany, and the Netherlands.

A signature Finkel wrote on a postcard in 1914 with a lead pencil, though obviously written in haste, has been acknowledged by the experts as the same handwriting as the military enlistment signatures of 1872 and the legal signature of 1921. So has Finkel's final signature—written three days before he died in August of 1930. The oddly Germanic F, the angle of slant, the heavy off-center dot on the i and the tight loops on the e and l were written by a feeble, failing hand—but it was the same hand that wrote "August Finckle" in Chicago in 1872.

"Same guy," said Chief Ydo. "It's consistent throughout."

The Last Look and The Final Analysis

When Frank Finkel sent his daughter a post card in 1914, and signed the marriage certificate that turned him from a hard-working stranger into a solid, prosperous citizen of Dayton in 1921, and signed his last will and testament in 1930, he signed as the Custer Survivor—Second Sergeant August Finckle, Company C, 7th Cavalry, last duty at the Little Big Horn. So indicated by records of the United States Army. And by a number of his fellow troopers in life, but never identified in death at the Little Big Horn battlefield by his best friend, Charles Windolph, who suffered pangs of remorse for the rest of his life because he couldn't give the "gallant soldier" a decent burial.

Whoever was buried under Finkel's marker at the Little Big Horn Battlefield Cemetery clearly wasn't the man who joined the U.S. Army in Chicago in January of 1872. The man who enlisted in Chicago, the man who helped Dayton grow into one of the prettiest towns in southern Washington, was buried in Dayton in 1930. His grave marker says: Frank Finkel.

Afterword

The Custer Myth describes doomed heroes battling it out to the last man, heroic in their final defiance. That did not happen. Several clusters of Custer's men rallied and fought, some around Custer himself, some around Myles Keogh, some on Calhoun Ridge. Those who had a chance tried to escape, in the case of C Company, after both officers disappeared. One man made it, Frank Finkel; however inadvertently, an escape it was. One can only contemplate his fate if a warrior's rifle shot had not smashed the stock of his carbine and another rifle shot, the flank of his sorrel.

But those things did happen and the two, man and horse, rushed along the shoreline of the Little Big Horn River into the cottonwood wilderness, escaping certain death.

The battle of the Little Big Horn continues to hold the interest of scholars, students, and aficionados of the event. Significant new information about it has been uncovered, the archaeological findings by Prof. Richard A. Fox of the University of South Dakota in the 1980s is a prime example. It was a close and revealing look at that event, one that illustrated the truth about the battle, a truth that ran counter to the illusion created by mythology.

Once again a truth contrary to mythology has been demonstrated. New information has resulted from the sifting of data, the examination of government and private documents, the use of established research, the search for signatures, and the inclusion of handwriting experts to determine fact. The finding has resulted in the illumination of a dark corner in the history of the battle at the Little Big Horn about a subject that has often initiated controversy: the reality of a soldier who survived the conflict. Handwriting analysis establishes that a soldier did survive. Frank Finkel, Second Sergeant of C Company was that soldier.

A half-dozen others were miles from the battlefield when they were caught and killed, and Nathan Short, a young man with only a year in the 7th Cavalry, was about 25 miles from the Little Big Horn when his horse fell on him and they died together.

Frank Finkel made it. He started to become a legend in his home town of Dayton, Washington when he muttered at an Exhibition at the Dreamland Theater, took a friend into his confidence, and finally told the world, at a horseshoe game in April of 1920, that he was a survivor of Custer's Last Stand and the battle wasn't what people thought it was.

Finkel wasn't the only voice raised to protest the myth of heroes cut down by savages in a Sioux ambush. His buddy, Charles Windolph, the longest-living survivor of the seven companies trapped on Reno Hill, summed it up: "…we knew you couldn't keep white men out of these hills once word of the gold discovery got out to the world.… All the soldiers in the United States couldn't hold back the tide then. You could sign all the Indian treaties you could pack on a mule, and they wouldn't do any good.… Custer got a lot of notoriety from his Black Hills expedition, and the discovery of gold. But he never had any luck after that."[1] Willam O. Taylor, another Reno Hill survivor, also blamed the "massacre" on the politicians, and to some extent on the officers. Neither man hated Indians.

Frank Finkel, the only survivor of Custer's five companies, agreed with them. His first wife was rumored to be part Indian herself, yet he loved and respected her and took great pride in their children, and he never had any stomach for the harum-scarum sideshows that depicted all Indians as mindless murderers and all soldiers as

The 7th Cavalry in an 1874 expedition in the Black Hills of the Dakota Territory

mythic heroes. He almost blew up at the misconstruction of the Last Stand at the Dreamland Theater during the war and the outburst at the horseshoe game in 1920, triggered by a one-sided version of the "massacre," made him a local celebrity in Dayton. He knew that the Little Big Horn was a surprise attack that failed because the government-licensed traders had sold the Indians better rifles than the War Department issued to him and his buddies. He didn't buy into the Custer Myth. Frank Finkel didn't think of himself as a hero. But his blunt honesty about what actually happened at the Little Big Horn, now that we know from forensic evidence that he was really there, make him a legend. He held it in a long time but he finally told the truth about Custer's Last Stand.

Notes
[1]Windolph, Charles, *I Fought With Custer,* page 42.

Bibliography

ADAMS, Alexander *SITTING BULL, AN EPIC OF THE PLAINS*, G.P. Putnam's Sons, NY, 1973

ALEXROD, Alan *CHRONICLE OF THE INDIAN WARS*, Prentice Hall, NJ, 1993

AMBROSE, Stephen *CRAZY HORSE AND CUSTER: The Parallel Lives of Two American Warriors*, Doubleday & Co., Garden City, NY, 1975

BARNETT, Louise *TOUCHED BY FIRE: The Life, Death and Mythic Afterlife of George Armstrong Custer*, Henry Holt and Co., NY, 1996

BASS, Althea *THE ARAPAHO WAY: A Memoir of an Indian Boyhood*, Clarkson Potter, Inc.,NY 1966

BOURKE, John G. *ON THE BORDER WITH CROOK*, University of Nebraska Press, Lincoln, Nebraska, 1971

BRADY, Cyrus T. *INDIAN FIGHTS AND FIGHTERS*, Bison Books, North Dakota, 1971   ISBN: 978-080 3257 436

BRININSTOOL, E.A. *FIGHTING INDIAN WARRIORS*, Bonanza Books, division of Crown Publishers, NY, 1953 LC: 53-7174

BRININSTOOL, E.A. *TROOPERS WITH CUSTER*, Stackpole Books, Mechanicsburg, PA   ISBN: 780811-717427

BROWN, Dee   *BURY MY HEART AT WOUNDED KNEE*: *An Indian History of the American West*, Holt, Rinehart & Winston, NY, 1971   ISBN 003085 3222

BROWN, Dee   *THE AMERICAN WEST*, Charles Scribner's Sons, NY, 1994   ISBN 0-02-517421-5

BROWN, DEE THE BEST OF DEE BROWN'S WEST, Clear Light Publishing, Santa Fe, New Mexico, 1998

BROWN, Dee   *THE GALVANIZED YANKEES*, University of Illinois Press, Urbana, 1963

BROWN, Joseph Epes. *THE SACRED PIPE*, University of Oklahoma Press, Norman, OK, 1953

CAMP, Walter Mason *CUSTER IN '76   Camp's notes on the Custer Fight*, edited by HAMMER, Kenneth, *CUSTER IN '76*, Brigham Young University Press, Provo, Utah, 1976 ISBN: 0-8425-0399-4

CAPPS, Benjamin *NATIVE AMERICANS OF THE OLD WEST*, Time/Life Books, NY, 1973/1995

CLARK, Robert A. *THE KILLING OF CHIEF CRAZY HORSE: Three Eyewitness Views*, University of Nebraska Press, Lincoln, Nebraska, 1976

COSGROVE, Bronwyn *THE COMPLETE HISTORY OF COSTUME AND FASHION*, Checkmark Books, New York, NY, 2000

CONNELL, Evan S. *SON OF THE MORNING STAR*, North Point Press, San Francisco, CA, 1984 ISBN: 0-86547-160-6

CUNNINGHAM, Eugene *TRIGGERNOMETRY; A GALLERY OF GUNFIGHTERS*, The Press of the Pioneers, Inc., NY, 1934

CUSTER, Elizabeth *BOOTS AND SADDLES or Life in Dakota with Gen. Custer*, Corner House Publisher, Williamstown, MA, 1885, 1974

CUSTER, Elizabeth *FOLLOWING THE GUIDON*, University of Oklahoma Press, Norman, OK, 1890, 1967

CUSTER, Elizabeth *TENTING ON THE PLAINS*, University of Oklahoma Press 1887, 1967

CUSTER, George A. *MY LIFE ON THE PLAINS*, edited by Milo Quaife, Bison Books, University of Nebraska Press, Lincoln, Nebraska, 1966 [original 1874]

DONOVAN, Jim *CUSTER AND THE LITTLE BIG HORN, The Man, the Mystery, the Myth*, Voyageur Press, 2001

EASTMAN, Charles A. *FROM THE DEEP WOODS TO CIVILIZATION*, R.R. Donnelley & Sons, Chicago, IL, 2001

FIELDER, Mildred *SIOUX INDIAN LEADERS*, Superior Publishing Co., Seattle, Washington, 1975 ISBN: 0-517-369540

FOX, Richard A. *ARCHAEOLOGY, HISTORY, AND CUSTER'S LAST BATTLE*, University of Oklahoma Press, Norman, OK, 1993 ISBN: 0-8061-2998- www.ou.edu/ou-press

GRANT, Ulysses S. III *ULYSSES S GRANT: Warrior and Statesman*, William Morrow & Co., NY, 1969

GRAHAM, W.A. *THE CUSTER MYTH*, Stackpole Books, Mechanicsburg, PA, 1953   ISBN: 780811-727266

HAGEDORN, Hermann *ROOSEVELT IN THE BAD LANDS*, Houghton Mifflin Co., Boston, MA, 1930

HALLAHAN, William H. *MISFIRE*, Charles Scribner's Sons, New York, New York, 1994 ISBN:0-684-19359-0

HASSRICK, Royal B. *THE SIOUX: Life and Customs of a Warrior Society*, University of Oklahoma Press, Norman, OK, 1964

HOIG, Stan *THE BATTLE OF THE WASHITA*, Doubleday & Co., Garden City, NY, 1976 ISBN 0-385-11274-2

HUSBY, Karla J. *UNDER CUSTER'S COMMAND*, The Civil War Journal Of James Henry Avery, Brassey's, Washington DC, 2000

JOSEPHY, Alvin M. Jr. *500 NATIONS*, Alfred A Knopf, NY, 1994

KEEGAN, John *FIELDS OF BATTLE: The Wars for North America*, Alfred Knopf, NY, 1996

KELLY, Fanny *NARRATIVE OF MY CAPTIVITY AMONG THE SIOUX INDIANS*, Konecky & Konecky, New York, New York, 1990   ISBN 1-56852-244-4 [copyright by R. R. Donnelley & Sons]

KENNEDY, Michael S. *THE RED MAN'S WEST*, Hastings House, NY, 1965

KENT, Zachary *GEORGE ARMSTRONG CUSTER, Civil Wear General and Western Legend, Enslow Publishers, Berkley Heights, NJ 2000*

KUHLMAN, Charles *LEGEND INTO HISTORY And DID CUSTER DISOBEY ORDERS AT THE BATTLE OF THE LITTE BIG HORN?*, Stackpole Books, Mechanicsburg, PA, 1957 ISBN: 780811-704533

LA FARGE, Olive *A PICTORIAL HISTORY OF THE AMERICAN INDIAN*, Crown Publishing, NY, 1956

LAMPMAN, Evelyn S. *ONCE UPON THE LITTLE BIG HORN*, Thomas Crowell Co., NY, 1971

LINDERMAN, Frank *PRETTY-SHIELD, Medicine Woman of the Crows*, John Day Co., NY, 1932, 1972

LOSSING, Benson J. *THE PICTORIAL FIELD BOOK OF THE REVOLUTION*, Charles Tuttle Co., Rutland, Vermont, 1859, 1972 reprint

MAILS, Thomas E. *THE MYSTIC WARRIORS OF THE PLAINS*, Doubleday, Garden City, NY, 1972

MARQUIS, Thomas B. *KEEP THE LAST BULLET FOR YOURSELF*, Two Continents Publishing Group, New York 1976

MARTIN, David G. *CARL BORNEMANN'S REGIMENT*, [published for Longstreet House by Gateway Press, Inc, Baltimore, MD, 1960] ISBN: 3-9510-2003-9157-4 LC: 86-82998

MARRIN, Albert *SITTING BULL AND HIS WORLD*, Dutton, NY, 2000

McFEELY, William S. *GRANT: A Biography*, W.W. Norton & Co., NY, London, 1981

McPHERSON, James *THE BATTLE CRY OF FREEDOM: The Civil War Era*, Oxford University Press, NY, 1988

McPHERSON, James *HALLOWED GROUND: A Walk at Gettysburg*, Crown Publishers, NY, 2003

MERINGTON, Marguerite *THE CUSTER STORY, The Life and Intimate Letters of General George A. Custer and His Wife Elizabeth*, Devin-Adair, New York, 1950

NADEAU, Remi *FORT LARAMIE AND THE SIOUX INDIANS*, Prentice-Hall, Englewood Cliffs, 1967

NEIHARDT, John G. *BLACK ELK SPEAKS*, William Morrow & Co., NY, 1932

PAINE, Albert B *THOMAS NAST: His Period and His Pictures*, Benjamin Blom Publisher, NY, 1966

PARKMAN, Francis, *THE OREGON TRAIL: Sketches of Prairie and Rocky Mountain Life*, The Hertiage Press, Danbury, CT. 1949

PARKMAN, Francis, *FRANCE AND ENGLAND IN NORTH AMERICA*, Viking Press, 1991

POWERS, William K. *CRAZY HORSE AND CUSTER*, for Children Incorporated, Columbus, OH 1968

REEDSTROM, Ernest L. *BUGLES, BANNERS AND WAR BONNETS*, Bonanza Books [original by Caxton Printers], NY, 1977   ISBN 0-517-60519-8

REUSSWIG, William *A PICTURE REPORT OF THE CUSTER FI*GHT, Hastings House, NY, 1967

ROBINSON, Charles III *A GOOD YEAR TO DIE: The Story of the Great Sioux War*, Random House, NY, 1995

ROSA, Joseph *WILD BILL HICKOK: The Man and His Myth*, University of Kansas Press, Lawrence, Kansas, 1996

SANDOZ, Mari *THE BATTLE OF THE LITTLE BIG HORN*, Aeonian Press, Mattituck, NY, 1966

SCHMITT, Martin [and Dee Brown] *FIGHTING INDIANS OF THE WEST*, Charles Scribner & Sons, NY, 1948

SCHOENBERGER, Dale T. *THE GUNFIGHTERS*, Caxton Printers, Caldwell, Idaho , 1971 ISBN: 87004-207-6 LB: 70-123583

SCHULTZ, Duane *MONTH OF THE FREEZING MOON: The Sand Creek Massacre*, St. Martin's Press, NY, 1990

SLOTKIN, Richard *GUNFIGHTER NATION: The Myth of the Frontier in Twentieth-Century America*, Atheneum, NY, 1992

SMITH, Jean Edward *GRANT*, Simon & Schuster, NY, 2001

STANDS IN TIMBER, John *CHEYENNE MEMORIES*, Yale University Press, New Haven, CT 1867

STILES, T.J. *WARRIORS AND PIONEERS*, [collected and edited], Dept. of History, University of Oregon, published by [Perigee Books], The Berkley Publishing Group, NY, 1996 ISBN; 780399-519888

TAYLOR, William O. *WITH CUSTER ON THE LITTLE BIG HORN*: Viking Penguin, NY, 1996   ISBN: 0-670-86803-5

TEBBEL, John & JENNISON, Keith *THE AMERICAN INDIAN WARS*, Bonanza Books, NY, 1960

TIRREL, Norma, MONTANA, Fodor's Guides, Random House, NY 2006

URWIN, Gregory J.W. *THE UNITED STATES CAVALRY: An Illustrated History*, Blandford Press, NY, 1983

UTLEY, Robert [and Wilcomb Washburn] *THE AMERICAN HERITAGE HISTORY OF THE INDIAN WARS*, American Heritage Publishing, NY, 1977

UTLEY, Robert *FRONTIER REGULARS: The United States Army and the Indians, 1866–1890* Macmillan, New York. 1973

UTLEY, Robert *THE LANCE AND THE SHIELD*: The Life And Times of Sitting Bull, Henry Holt and Co., NY, 1993

VIOLA, Herman J. *LITTLE BIG HORN REMEMBERED*, Rivilo Books [Random House], NY, 1999

WALKER, Dale L. *LEGENDS & LIES*, A Forge Book, [published by Tom Doherty Assoc.], NY, 1997 ISBN: 0-312-86311-X

WALLACE, David Rains *THE BONEHUNTER'S REVENGE*, Houghton Mifflin Co., Boston, 1999

WEEMS, John E. *DEATH SONG: The Last of the Indian Wars*, Doubleday, Garden City, NY, 1976

WELCH, James [with Paul Stekler] *KILLING CUSTER*, W.W. Norton & Co., NY, 1994

WERT, Jeffry *CUSTER: The Controversial Life of George Armstrong Custer*, Simon & Schuster, NY, 1996

WERT, Jeffry *THE SWORD OF LINCOLN: The Army of the Potomac*, Simon & Schuster, NY, 2005

WETMORE, Helen C. *BUFFALO BILL: Last of the Great Scouts*, Bison Books, University of Nebraska Press, 1899, 1965, Lincoln, Nebraska

WORMSER, Richard E. *THE YELLOWLEGS: The Story of the U.S. Cavalry*, Doubleday, Garden City, NY, 1966

MAGAZINES

AMERICAN HERITAGE

KOSTER, John P. *THE FORTY-DAY SCOUT*, June/July 1980, (Illustrated by Dennis Lyatt)

MILLER, David H. *ECHOS OF THE LITTLE BIG HORN*, American Heritage Magazine, June, 1971 [pp.28-40]

VESTAL, Stanley THE MAN WHO KILLED CUSTER, February 1957

NEW JERSEY HERITAGE

MAPPEN, Marc *LAST SECRET OF THE LAST STAND*, Winter, 2006, Vol. 5, Issue 1. Montclair, NJ, 2006

WINNERS OF THE WEST

June. 1939 Issue, St. Louis, Missouri, Letters Column, Hermie's Request For Information on Frank Finkel /Frank Hall.

INTERNET

FEDERICI, Richard SGT. DANIEL KANIPE, Mohican Press, www.mohicanpress.com/battles/ba04004.html, 1995

YOUNG, Steve PISTOL LINKS OHIO MAN TO BATTLE VET, Argus Leader, www.argusleader.com/specialsections/2001/bighorn/mondayarticle2.shtml

MEN WITH THE SEVENTH CAVALRY At the Time of the Battle, Little Big Horn Associates, www.lbha.org/Cavalry/NameA.htm

www.custerslaststand.org/source/rainface.html

REFERENCE

AMERICAN NATIONAL BIOGRAPHY, edited by Jon A. Garraty, Oxford University Press, NY and Oxford, 1999

APPLETON'S CYCLOPAEDIA OF AMERICAN BIOGRAPHY, edited by James Grant Wilson and John Fiske, Appleton & Co., NY, 1895

BIOGRAPHICAL DIRECTORY OF THE UNITED STATES CONGRESS, 1774-1989, US Government Printing Office, Washington, DC., 1989

CURRENT BIOGRAPHY, editors of 1940 and 1944.

DICTIONARY OF AMERICAN BIOGRAPHY, edited by Allen Johnson, Charles Scribner's Sons, NY, 1964

THE NATIONAL CYCLOPAEDIA OF AMERICAN BIOGRAPHY, James T. White & Co., NY, 1898

WHO WAS WHO IN AMERICA, Marquis Publication, vol. 2, Chicago, IL, 1950

PROCEEDINGS OF THE HOUSE OF REPRESENTATIVES RELATING TO THE IMPEACHMENT OF W.W, BELKNAP, LATE SECRETARY OF WAR. Government Printing Office, Washington DC, 1876.

MUSEUMS and COLLECTIONS

Oshkosh Public Museum
1331 Algoma Boulevard
Oshkosh, Wisconsin 54902-2799
(The Frank Finkle Collection)

Chester Fritz Library
University of North Dakota
PO Box 9000
Grand Forks, North Dakota 58202
(Charles Kuhlman's Finkel Narrative)

City of Oshkosh Assessor's Office
216 Church Avenue
PO Box 1130
Oshkosh, Wisconsin 54903-1130
(Hermie Billmeyer Death Cerificate)

Office of the Auditor
Columbia County, Washington
Sharon D. Richter, Auditor
341 E. Main Street,
Dayton, Washington 99328
(Finkel's marriage papers, land transactions, wills, death certificate, burial record)

Idaho State Historical Society
1109 Main Street
Boise, Idaho 83702-5642
(Frank and Ben Finkel family papers based on U.S. Census, newspapers)

Kansas State Historical Society
Reference Section
Center For Historical Research
6425 SW 6th Avenue,
Topeka, Kansas 66615-1099

Utah History Research Center
300 S. Rio Grande Street
Salt Lake City, Utah 84101-1182

Winnebago County Courthouse
Registrar of Deeds Office
PO Box 2808
Oshkosh, Wisconsin 54903

Forderverein
Deutsches Auswanderermuseum e.V.
Inselstrasse 6
27568 Bremerhaven
Germany
(Immigration records from German states to United States)

Geheimes Staatsarchiv
Preussische Kulturbesitz
Archivstrasse 12/14
D14195 Berlin (Dahlem)
Germany
(Prussian Army military records)

Index

For the sake of consistency references to Frank Finkel and his immediate relatives appear under "Finkel" although "Finckel" and "Finkle" also appear in the text. Page numbers followed by *ph* indicate a photograph, those followed by an n indicate an endnote, and those followed by *m* indicate a map.

About The Author

John Koster has written about the U.S. Cavalry and American Indians in *American Heritage*, Custer's Last Stand in *National Geographic*, *Wild West* and for the British Marshall Cavendish syndicate. He has also written articles for *American History*, *America's Civil War*, *Civil War Times Illustrated*, and *Military History* and in U.S. Army publications including *Infantry* and *Soldiers*. An award-winning writer in history, journalism, and sociology, Koster has lectured at Rutgers, Long Island University, and Fairlegh Dickinson, and taught writing for publication as an adjunct professor at Ramapo College. He has also written on business matters ranging from agriculture to real estate. He is a veteran of the United States Army.

His journalism awards include the SDX for Distinguished Public Service, the AAA Highway Safety Award, two nominations for the NJPA Award, and one for the Ernie Pyle Award. A newspaperman since the late 1960s, he has covered the spectrum of local government, politics, and war crimes investigations.

Photo; Author with archivist Minjae Kim